D0296973

£3.95

Buses
annual

Edited by Gavin Booth

LONDON
IAN ALLAN LTD

981

Acknowledgements

The photographs and illustrations in *Buses Annual 1981* were supplied by:

John Aldridge: 92-97
G. H. F. Atkins: 56-60
Berliet: 45
Gavin Booth: Cover, 29, 42, 43, 44, 47, 89, 90, 110, 111
Stewart J. Brown: 64-68
G. Coxon: 20 (bottom), 30-34, 79 (centre), 81, 83 (top)
Michael Dryhurst: 19 (bottom)
Michael Dryhurst Collection: 80
Michael Dryhurst, courtesy David Wootton: 83 (centre, bottom), 85, 86
M. Fowler: 5-10, 61 (centre), 77
John Gascoine: 28
Richard Gillespie: 25 (top, centre)
D. Fereday Glenn: 35-39, 79 (top), 114 (bottom)
Roger Hyslop: 21, 23 (top, centre), 25 (bottom)

Robert E. Jowitt: 62 (bottom), 98-103
David Kaye: 75, 76
Eamonn Kentell: 23 (bottom), 27
Leyland Vehicles: 108
Lincolnshire: 78
G. R. Mills: 17 (top, bottom), 19 (top, centre), 20 (top, centre), 61 (bottom), 62 (centre), 69-73, 115 (centre)
Alan Millar: 117-121
T. W. Moore: 1, 3, 18 (top), 46, 61 (top), 62 (top), 91, 112 (centre), 114 (top), 115 (bottom), 122-129
Don Morris: 115 (top)
A. Moyes: 17 (centre), 48-55
National Bus Company: 74
Allen T. Smith: 104-107
Viewfinder: 109, 112 (bottom), 113
Willowbrook: 40, 41
R. L. Wilson: 11-16, 18 (centre, bottom), 79 (bottom), 114 (centre)
A. N. Wolstenholme: Endpapers

Cover: Only 50 AEC/Park Royal Routemasters were sold outside London and were delivered to Northern General in 1964/65 — although some of these have recently found homes in London. One of Northern's 1965 Routemasters on the Tyne Bridge, Newcastle, in 1979.

Front endpapers: The line and scraper-board artwork of A. N. Wolstenholme graced the covers and pages of Ian Allan publications in the 1940s and 1950s. The selection at the front of the *Annual* are from the 1948 East Kent ABC, showing a 1947 Leyland Tiger/Park Royal coach; a Birmingham City Transport RT-type AEC Regent III/Park Royal of 1947, from the 1950 ABC of BCT buses; and a 1948 Leyland PD1/ECW from the 1949 ABC of Bristol Tramways vehicles.

Previous pages: A Leicester City Transport MCW Metropolitan pauses under the Clock Tower after the rush hour one evening in January 1977. Other examples of T. W. Moore's night photography appear on pages 122-129.

Right: Cheltenham Coach Station has long been recognised as a mecca for enthusiasts, here watching the arrival of a Black & White Leopard/Duple.

First published 1980

ISBN 0 7110 1047 1

Published by Ian Allan Ltd, Shepperton, Surrey; and printed by Ian Allan Printing Ltd at their works at Coombelands in Runnymede, England

About BUSES

This Annual carries the name of the popular monthly magazine which has, for many years, met the needs of both the PSV industry and its many enthusiast followers. If you find this Annual interesting you may care to place a regular order for BUSES through your newsagent or book an annual subscription through the publisher, IAN ALLAN LTD, Subscriptions Department, Terminal House, Shepperton TW17 8AS.

Contents

Introduction

'England', wrote George Santayana, 'is the paradise of individuality, eccentricity, heresy, anomalies, hobbies and humours'. And if, like so many others, by 'England' he really meant 'Britain' — something those of us who are not English find hard to forgive — then his comment is at least accurate about our national characteristics.

And if our particular eccentricity is an interest in road passenger transport, then it is an interest to be enjoyed; it is that sense of enjoyment that I try to reflect in *Buses Annual* each year. Traditionally *Annual* readers are a mixture of enthusiasts and professionals — enthusiastic professionals, perhaps — and the articles in the 1981 edition are directed at this mixed audience.

The tone of the contributions is sometimes light-hearted. Stewart Brown's memories of Aberdeen, and Robert Jowitt's romantic recollections of electric traction in Bournemouth, Leeds and Sheffield, fall into that category. Tony Moyes looks back to South Wales as it was in the 1960s; Alan Millar describes how the manufacturing industry misjudged the market for rear-engined single-deckers; Michael Dryhurst remembers the BET fleets that have disappeared under the cloak of rationalisation; David Fereday Glenn describes a trip to Devon in a Bristol LHS.

Coming to more recent events, there is an article on Motor Shows in the 1970s, Michael Fowler and Tony Peart on South Yorkshire PTE's individual policies, David Kaye on Community Buses, Ray Stenning on Plaxton's Panorama coach body and its successors, and Lawrie Bowles on London Transport's recent problems.

As usual, the pictorial content of the *Annual* is of equal importance. Regular contributors include Reg Wilson, travelling from Cambria north to Cumbria; Geoffrey Atkins on the Yorkshire Woollen fleet; Geoff Mills on independents in the South Midlands; another Geoffrey — Coxon — on independents in Northumbria; and award-winning photographer Tom Moore demonstrates the art of night photography. Elsewhere there are photo-features on new buses in older liveries, on tow wagons and on Scotland 30 years ago, and our overseas feature goes further afield this year, to South America with John Aldridge.

So, to use an old Scots phrase, a mixter-maxter — a miscellaneous jumble — though not, I hope the 'confused mixture' suggested in an alternative definition! Welcome to *Buses Annual 1981*.

Gavin Booth
Edinburgh

4

An Independent Line

An SYPTE Roe-bodied
Leyland Atlantean in
Birley Moor Road,
Sheffield.

**Of Britain's Passenger Transport Executives,
South Yorkshire has pursued some very
independent policies. TONY PEART and
MICHAEL FOWLER look at the development
of the PTE — best-known to many for cheap
fares and articulated buses**

South Yorkshire is a new county of some 600 square
miles and 1.3million inhabitants, formed under the
revision of boundaries scheme of 1974. The South
Yorkshire PTE serves much of this area, although
interestingly, Barnsley, which is the administrative
centre of the county, is served by the NBC subsidiary
company Yorkshire Traction, which has its headquarters there. The transport systems of Sheffield,
Rotherham and Doncaster, the other three major
centres of population in the area, were all absorbed by
the PTE on 1 April 1974, and its three districts are
administered from the head offices of the constituents,
with the Sheffield Exchange Street office as the headquarters of the PTE itself. Topographically South
Yorkshire is an extremely varied county. The eastern

side is flat, rich agricultural or fenland country, while
the west includes the foothills of the Pennines. Between
these extremes is much lovely countryside, although
industry is never far away, and it is still possible to see
how spectacularly beautiful the vale of the Don once
was. The area is of tremendous historical and
archaelogical interest, and to the transport enthusiast
has always been a prime attraction.

The bus fleets absorbed reflected the terrain in the
areas served by the operators. Sheffield had operated
three fleets, known as A, B and C until the end of
1969. The A fleet was purely Sheffield Corporation-
owned; B was owned jointly by the Corporation and
British Railways (formerly LMS and LNE Railways);
and C was railway-owned. Postwar policy had been to
use buses with large engines, since much of the
territory worked was hilly, and AECs and Leylands
became predominant. First Atlanteans, and later
Fleetlines, were purchased in large numbers from
1959. The 1968 Transport Act ensured the end of the
tri-partite arrangement, and Sheffield Corporation
purchased the B services and vehicles but were not
able to purchase all the C routes, some of which

remained jointly operated, while others went to the National Bus Company along with most of the vehicles, although many did remain in Sheffield for some time on hire. Rotherham, too, had hills to contend with, and for many years purchased Bristol motor buses almost exclusively, with the Gardner 5 cylinder engine as standard. After a period when the Crossley DD42 was purchased in numbers, Rotherham opted for Daimlers, and the CVG6 became the typical Rotherham bus before the introduction of the Daimler Fleetline. Doncaster's policy had never been one of standardisation, at least during the 1930s, 1940s and 1950s and although by the 1970s there was a definite shift towards the operation of Gardner-engined vehicles, Doncaster provided perhaps the greatest number of odd types proportionate to the size of the undertaking, but, as with Rotherham, the most modern double-deckers were Daimler Fleetlines, Atlanteans being definitely eschewed by both undertakings. Sheffield provided over 680 buses on formation of the PTE, Doncaster some 125 and Rotherham 135. There were of course, numerous ancillary vehicles as well.

All three operators had attractive liveries. Sheffield buses were a pale cream with three bands of ultramarine (officially classed as azure blue), and black beading. The scheme was saved from a feeling of coldness by the imaginative use of bright red for the wheels, although from the mid 1960s blue wheels were used when a Conservative council was in power, red when a Labour council ruled. Rotherham had a slightly less elaborate scheme of broad bands of medium blue and cream, the latter darker than Sheffield's. Wheels were black. While Sheffield's livery had remained much the same for 40 years, with the exception of a mercifully short-lived experiment with green in the 1950s, Rotherham's had materially altered, from the use of a near Prussian blue, with swoops, to the royal blue used from the 1950s. Doncaster's traditional colours were dark crimson lake and white, but under the aegis of Mr Tom Bamford the crimson lake became cherry red and the three white bands were abandoned in favour of just one, above the lower deck windows. Doncaster's final livery, adopted by the undertaking's last manager, R. R. Davies, was a startling scheme of cherry red with a mauve stripe on two levels, the stripe being surrounded by white bands; wheels were red. The scheme sounds garish, but in practice was very effective.

One of the first effects of PTE policy was the institution of a corporate livery, and to obviate bickering from the representatives of the PTEs constituent towns, this was to be completely new. To say that the new colours were greeted with mixed reactions would be putting it mildly, and in general the new livery was viewed with dismay. The fact that the PTE has modified it on two occasions since its introduction (and carried out various livery experiments) suggests that even in official circles there has not been universal approbation. The earliest vehicles repainted emerged in cream with the roof and the skirt in a most insipid pale brown. Loosely termed 'coffee and cream', the livery inspired several wags to remark that someone had been over-liberal with the milk. The use of black relief was, however, attractive, but this obviously was too expensive and was rapidly abandoned. The brown was soon deepened to something like a chestnut shade, and it was interesting to see that on the early re-paints weathering caused the cream to become ivory and the tan to become an indescribable pinkish colour. In late 1978 the tan had become a much darker brown, but somehow still of a rather odd shade. Red wheels are perhaps the most attractive part of the scheme, but a South Yorkshire PTE vehicle has usually lost its 'edge' after being out of the paint shops for a few days, and public reaction seems to be, at best, one of rather grudging acceptance rather than enthusiasm. There were still ex-Sheffield buses running in cream and blue in 1979 and Doncaster had one single-decker repainted in the Davies 'humbug' livery in connection with the 75th anniversary of the town's transport department, Rotherham's blue and cream also lasted until 1979, although the two survivors, both CVG6/30s, were at the Doncaster depot. During 1979 those buses still retaining Sheffield livery had their blue bands and Sheffield insignia painted out in a 'crash' programme. The result was ghostly and gave a slight feeling of unreality. Some of these vehicles were given a tan skirt, however.

Just as a certain amount of uncertainty was manifest when the executive's new livery was being chosen, so a similar indecision showed itself in the emblems and insignia which were to adorn the sides of the newly repainted cream and tan buses. Early repaints bore the new county's emblem, a stylised white rose flowering above the letters SY, representing foliage, and encircled by the executive's title with a larger South Yorkshire alongside, of weak design and in the county's colours of green and purple. The effect was unhappy, and although the rose emblem (without its accompanying title) is still used on the nearside of vehicles, the green and purple fleetname soon disappeared. For a brief and pleasant interlude the county's handsome coat of arms was used, but on relatively few buses, before it was superseded by the executive's new logotype, which, like many such, needs careful study before it means anything at all, a fact which was amusingly underlined when a panel with the logo emblazoned on it was mounted upside down outside Barnsley bus station; unfortunately

The distinctive lines of one of the Van Hool-McArdle bodied Ailsas in the centre of Sheffield.

someone in authority noticed — the county's administrative headquarters are only a few yards away. By the late 1970s the insignia had become standardised, with the white rose and executive's logo appearing on each vehicle, with lettering 'South Yorkshire Transport' in an italic style and in a brown-gold colour, although in 1979 buses began to appear with a simplified version of the logo and black lettering in an upright style. Originally bus numbers were in gold, which was illegible against the cream background colour, but again by the end of the decade black numbers were universal.

The area in which the South Yorkshire PTE operates its services is one which has traditionally been a stronghold of prosperous independent operators, and the PTE was not long in declaring its intention of taking these operators over. Apart from this independent operation within its area, the executive does not have a monopoly by any means, and the National Bus Company plays a significant part in providing South Yorkshire's bus services. Undoubtedly the most important NBC operator is Yorkshire Traction, since this is based within the PTE's territory, with the company's 340 vehicles shared between the headquarters at Barnsley and other depots at Doncaster, Rawmarsh, Wombwell, Shafton and Huddersfield, the last being within the area served by the West Yorkshire PTE. Services are fully co-ordinated with those of the two PTEs. Of the other NBC companies, East Midland has several routes terminating in South Yorkshire. Lincolnshire, Trent, Potteries and the West Riding Group all work into the county and even Ribble has a small stake in the area's transport.

The South Yorkshire PTE was not long in implementing its declared policy of absorbing independent operators. The first to be swallowed up was Booth and Fisher, at Halfway, with a fleet of nearly 40 vehicles, just over a year after the executive was formed. The Booth and Fisher company, with its fleet of single-deck AECs and Albions, functioned as a separate entity for some time, but very gradually the red and cream colours disappeared and vehicles from other parts of the PTE were drafted in. The story of Booth and Fisher was told in *Buses* 256 in July 1976. Two independents remain, working into Sheffield: A. & C. Wigmore, with a service from Dinnington, and Dearneways, with a limited-stop service from Thurnscoe. Chesterfield Transport and the West Yorkshire PTE operate routes into Sheffield centre too, while Baddeley Brothers, also

The PTE's East Lancs-bodied Foden, bought for evaluation, near Jordanthorpe terminus.

Leaving Greenland depot, Sheffield, East Lancs-bodied Dennis Dominator 521, with Rolls-Royce engine. A further 144 Dominators were ordered late in 1979.

now part of the West Yorkshire PTE, has a route which terminates at Deepcar, on the outskirts of the city.

Rotherham has never been noted for independent operators and Dearneways is the only one with a route through the town, whilst Barnsley, once rich in such operators, has a sole survivor in South Yorkshire Road Transport, with a route which terminates there, L. Pepper and Sons having gone to Yorkshire Traction in 1978 (*Buses* 279, June 1978).

Doncaster, with its abundance of independents, lost Felix Motors to the PTE in 1976. (*Buses Special* 1976). The AEC double-deckers were phased out; the Daimler Fleetlines, with the exception of one, went to Rotherham, and the AEC Reliances gradually passed to Booth and Fisher. Blue Ensign followed two years later, but this time the three Daimler Fleetlines and three Bedford coaches were retained by the Doncaster division. 1979 saw the disappearance of three more independent companies: T. Severn and Sons, Blue Line and Reliance, but the Severn depot at Dunscroft, a commodious and modern garage, is being retained as a

PTE bus depot. (*Buses* 292, July 1979). At the time of writing Rossie Motors, Leon Motors, Premier and South Yorkshire Road Transport continued to operate independently into Doncaster, which fortunately still has a diversity of companies with services into the town. Another independent to disappear recently was United Services, now part of the West Yorkshire PTE. There remains to be mentioned Selwyn Motors, with one Saturday journey into the town from South Humberside.

There were outstanding orders to be fulfilled when the PTE was formed and for some time there were deliveries of buses to Sheffield, Rotherham, Doncaster and Felix orders, although these were all Daimler Fleetlines. Some were delivered with Leyland engines, however, and three brand-new Atlanteans ordered by independent operators but not delivered were snapped up by the PTE. Leyland Leopards with Alexander Y-type bodies, the standard Sheffield express vehicle, continued to appear, but a new type of single-decker was the Leyland National, which, since the formation of the PTE, has been delivered in both A and B ver-

Above: An ex-Rotherham Daimler CVG6LX/30, with Roe body, working for the PTE in Doncaster.

Above right: A Roe-bodied Daimler Fleetline from the Felix fleet, still in Felix colours, at Adwick le Street, on the Skellow-Doncaster service.

Right: Doncaster's first rear-engined double-deckers were two 1967 Daimler Fleetlines with Roe bodies, and 1209 is seen on SYPTE service in 1977, approaching Doncaster along Thorne Road.

Below: In 1979 this ex-Sheffield Park Royal-bodied Fleetline was still operating in a 'livery' of all-over white — the Sheffield blue bands had simply been painted out.

sions. After a number of demonstrators had appeared, four Metropolitans ordered by Sheffield were delivered and orders were placed for no fewer than 62 Ailsas, whose distinctive screams added a new sound to the South Yorkshire roads. Orders were also placed for further Fleetlines, for Atlantean AN68s and Metrobuses. Odd men out — two Dennis Dominators and a Foden NC — are also operated, but orders have been placed for another 144 Dominators, with two more from a previous Blue Line order still to be delivered at the time of writing.

The SYPTE has become noted for its readiness to experiment with new types of vehicle and one such experiment has concerned electric buses. The two Crompton Parkinson 1972 battery buses CWO 516K and CWO 600K were purchased. EX61, the Greater Manchester Seddon Chloride 'Silent Rider' (XVU 387M), was operated spasmodically and Greater Manchester EX62 (GNC 276N), the Lucas vehicle, was used quite extensively and apparently successfully. Most of the experiments with electric traction were carried out in Doncaster. Greater interest was aroused nationally by the executive's trials with articulated vehicles and intention of using such buses on the Sheffield City Clipper Service. Volvo, MAN and Leyland DAB articulated buses were examined and an order placed for MAN and Leyland DAB types. So far as more conventional buses are concerned, the PTE has had a number of demonstrators, as well as showing a readiness to take unusual vehicles into stock, so that the fleet always contains some highly individualistic machines. The executive's particular concern with transmission systems, in particular the Voith type, has resulted in a number of departures from what might be termed the standard

product operating elsewhere, and such buses as the kneeling National have aroused great interest. A Leyland Atlantean powered by liquid petroleum gas is currently the subject of a further experiment.

Linkline is the title bestowed on the South Yorkshire rail network which British Rail and the PTE operate. Train fares are pegged and diesel multiple units bear the PTE logo, although the working of these trains is by no means confined to South Yorkshire.

The most controversial aspects of PTE policy do not concern vehicles at all, but stem from the County Council's insistence on cheap fares, resulting in the SYPTE being at loggerheads with whatever government is in power. Fares are subsidised from the rates, and although this does undoubtedly encourage use of the buses, it may result in the area's rates being unacceptably high. There is also a low children's fare in operation and free passes (with certain limitations on use) for old age pensioners. Socially much of the executive's policy seems laudable, but in the prevailing financial climate perhaps not entirely practicable. Less controversial is the executive's publicity policy. The issue of a most admirable map of services, with helpful leaflets and circulars is of inestimable value to the travelling public and must be considered one of the greatest benefits conferred by the establishment of the PTE; other proclaimed advantages have unfortunately proved theoretical rather than real.

In compiling this account the writers would like to record their gratitude for the help afforded by Mr Paul Beardsley of the South Yorkshire PTE.

One of the pioneering SYPTE MAN articulated buses on the 500 City Clipper service, in Commercial Street in January 1980.

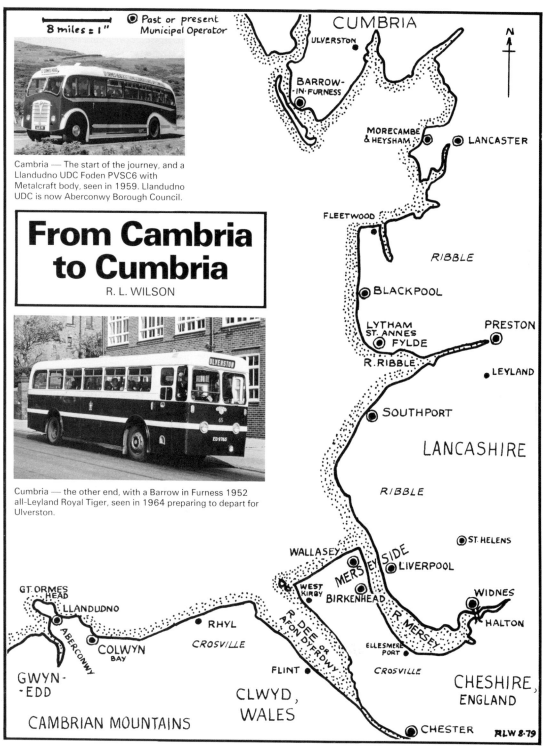

8 miles = 1"

⊚ Past or present
Municipal Operator

Cambria — The start of the journey, and a Llandudno UDC Foden PVSC6 with Metalcraft body, seen in 1959. Llandudno UDC is now Aberconwy Borough Council.

From Cambria to Cumbria

R. L. WILSON

Cumbria — the other end, with a Barrow in Furness 1952 all-Leyland Royal Tiger, seen in 1964 preparing to depart for Ulverston.

N

CUMBRIA

ULVERSTON

BARROW-IN-FURNESS

MORECAMBE & HEYSHAM ⊚ LANCASTER

FLEETWOOD

RIBBLE

⊚ BLACKPOOL

LYTHAM ST.ANNES ⊚ FYLDE   ⊚ PRESTON

R.RIBBLE

• LEYLAND

⊚ SOUTHPORT

LANCASHIRE

RIBBLE

⊚ ST.HELENS

WALLASEY

MERSEYSIDE ⊚ LIVERPOOL

WEST KIRBY   ⊚ BIRKENHEAD   WIDNES

R. MERSEY   HALTON

ELLESMERE PORT

CROSVILLE

CHESHIRE, ENGLAND

GT.ORMES HEAD

LLANDUDNO   • RHYL

ABERCONWY

COLWYN BAY   CROSVILLE

R. DEE OR AFON DYFRDWY

FLINT •

GWYN--EDD

CLWYD, WALES

CAMBRIAN MOUNTAINS

⊚ CHESTER   RLW 8·79

11

Colwyn Bay BC (now just Colwyn BC) operated this 1954 petrol-engined Bedford OLAZ with 21-seat Spurling body. It is seen at Colwyn Bay pier in 1955.

The main operator in North Wales is Crosville, which in 1977 was using this Bristol Lodekka LD6G on the Sea Front Service from Prestatyn to Pensarn; it is seen near Rhyl.

Below: Chester City Transport operated several Foden double-deckers. This 1949 Massey-bodied Foden PVD6 is seen in 1961 in Bridge Street, with the famous Rows in the background.

Wallasey Corporation, now part of Merseyside PTE, operated this unusual Bedford J2/Duple 19-seater, new in 1967. It is seen in 1967 on a shoppers route.

Birkenhead Corporation also disappeared into Merseyside PTE. This 1949 Guy Arab III with 56-seat Massey body is shown in 1960 at the Woodchurch Road roundabout.

Widnes Corporation, now Halton Transport, operated this 1949 all-Leyland PD2/1 in 1968, when it is seen against the background of the Widnes bridge over the River Mersey.

At Liverpool's famous Pier Head terminus, in 1961, a 1956 Liverpool Corporation Leyland Royal Tiger PSU1/13 with Crossley/LCPT 40-seat body. Alongside is Irish Cross-Channel boat bus PKD 589, an AEC Regal III with Roe body.

Southport's Lord Street bus station was converted from the old Cheshire Lines railway station. In 1967, a new Ribble Leyland Leopard PSU3/4R with Plaxton Panorama 45-seat body is seen under the ornate arches.

Preston Corporation was, naturally perhaps, a staunch Leyland user, and this all-Leyland Titan PD2/10, seen in 1967, was new in 1952. It is shown in Fishergate, before the impressive new central bus station was built.

J. Fishwick & Sons, the famous Leyland independent, is represented by this 1963 Leyland Atlantean PDR1/1 with lowheight MCW body, photographed in 1967.

Another early lowheight Atlantean/MCW, the former demonstrator 661 KTJ working with the independent Bamber Bridge Motor Services. The Atlantean passed to Ribble with the Bamber Bridge business in 1967.

Again a former Leyland demonstrator, 398 JTB was bought by Scout Motor Services of Preston. It was a normal-height Atlantean PDR1/1 with MCW body. It is seen at the old Preston bus station in 1961, and passed to Ribble in 1961 when the Scout business was acquired; the Scout fleetname was retained until 1968.

To complete a page of Atlanteans, a 1961 Standerwick Gay Hostess coach, with 50-seat Weymann body, in Preston in 1962. Standerwick, founded in 1908, was taken over by Ribble in 1932, but the name was retained for its goodwill value, and only disappeared when Standerwick and North Western were merged to form National Travel (North West).

Now Fylde Borough, Lytham St Annes
Corporation was famous for its gearless
Leylands, like this 1937 Titan TD5c, with
full-front Leyland 54-seat body, seen
leaving the depot in 1963, when it was
26 years old.

Blackpool's buses have tended to be less
well-known than the tramcars. This 1940
Leyland Tiger TS8, seen turning on to the
Promenade in 1962, had a Burlingham
34-seat centre-entrance body to a
particularly Blackpool style.

Lancaster Corporation was merged with
Morecambe and Heysham Corporation to
form the new Lancaster City Council fleet.
Representing the old Lancaster fleet are
three Crossley DD42/5s, the bus nearest
the camera being 569, with Crossley
56-seat body, new in 1947. They are seen
at Lancaster bus station in 1964.

New Wine in Old Bottles

An interesting recent development has been the appearance of current buses wearing older liveries — with differing degrees of success.

Top: Celebrating East Midland's golden jubilee in 1977, an Alexander-bodied Atlantean PDR1/2, in the one-time brown, cream and ochre livery, at Worksop.

Centre left: In the mid-1930s dark red Potteries livery, lowbridge MCW-bodied Atlantean 766 celebrates 100 years of public road transport in the Potteries.

Left: Blackburn celebrated its golden jubilee in 1979 by painting this Atlantean AN68A/1R with East Lancs body in the original green livery.

To commemorate 75 years of Midland Red, D12 6007 was repainted in the old BET-style livery. This Fleetline/Alexander is seen taking visitors to the Royal Showground at Stoneleigh.

For its 'Big Bus Show' in September 1979, Merseyside PTE repainted a number of its buses in the liveries of its former constituents. This Leyland Atlantean/MCW, seen near Hoylake Station, wears the former Wallasey Corporation 1929 tramway livery of yellow-green and cream.

Another 1929 tramway livery on a Merseyside PTE bus — a 1974 Leyland Atlantean AN68/1R with Alexander body. The livery is the maroon and cream of Birkenhead Corporation.

In Plymouth tram-style red-brown and cream, Atlantean/Park Royal 79 celebrates Plymouth's 50 years as a city, at the 1979 Hillingdon Showbus Rally.

Single-deckers in old liveries are less common. This Gosport & Fareham Bristol RELL6G/ECW 44-seater recalls the former independent Provincial fleetname and green livery.

Southampton painted this 1965 AEC Regent V into an attractive blue, white and grey livery to commemorate 100 years of municipal transport, in 1979.

London Transport's 1979 resurrection of the 1829 Shillibeer Omnibus livery was mainly applied to Routemasters, but the bus advertising Leyland Vehicles Ltd was, appropriately, a Park Royal-bodied Leyland Fleetline B20 — in fact DM2646, numerically the last of London's Fleetlines.

One of the more bizarre liveries was that conceived by Thamesdown Transport to celebrate the 75th anniversary of its predecessor Swindon Corporation Tramways. Fleetline/ECW 75 is seen in Park Lane, London, in 1979.

Three Tyne & Wear PTE buses were painted in Sunderland Corporation liveries to mark the centenary of local public transport in the town. Fleetline/Alexander 807 is seen in the post-1952 green and cream livery.

Bullseye off Target?

London Transport's fortunes in the 1970s were mixed. The problems with the Daimler Fleetlines (DMS1 is seen above) and other 'off-the-peg' buses have been well documented. LAWRIE BOWLES looks back.

During the 1960s, it had become increasingly clear to London Transport's planners that costs of operation were becoming progressively greater than the revenue from the buses. More important, attracting staff was becoming very difficult, and retaining the staff was just as hard. So it was therefore decided that one-man operation of bus services on a wide scale was a way of improving the service to the public. From November 1964, RFs had been allowed to operate as one-man buses in the suburban areas, but LT's plans to convert more central routes to OMO required the use of larger, standee single-deckers since the authorities would not permit one-man operated double-deckers at that time.

To implement its *Reshaping London's Buses* plan, published in 1966, LT ordered a fleet of AEC Swift single-deckers in several batches, eventually totalling 665 units for central and country use. This was the MB family, known as Merlins. Some went into use in 1966 on experimental express Red Arrow route 500, but entry into service of the others had to wait until late in 1968 following protracted negotiation with the Transport & General Workers' Union.

It was soon found that the 36ft length of the Merlins was too great for easy manoeuvring around London's narrow streets and caused serious capacity problems in garages, so follow-up orders were for a 33ft long version of the Swift, which retained this name in LT use. 838 of these were ordered for both country and central areas, and the Merlins and Swifts marked the departure from traditional London Transport practice in that they were not specifically developed for use in London, but were merely an adaptation of a standard vehicle.

Meanwhile, the last of the Routemasters had been delivered in February 1968 against the background that the Reshaping Plan forecast the end of crew operation in London within seven to eight years with the consequent demise of these fine vehicles. The RM, having ousted London's trolleybuses by 1962, then replaced the RTWs, RTLs and the oldest-bodied RTs by 1970. Thus at the start of the 1970s, the RM and RT still reigned supreme, but the MB family was all in service, and the first of the SMs (Swifts) was due in January 1970.

The traditional LT vehicle was of course a double-decker, and following a relaxation of restrictions in the late 1960s, permission to operate single-manned double-deckers in central London was forthcoming. LT had purchased 50 Leyland Atlanteans and 8 Daimler Fleetlines for crew operation in 1965/66 to compare rear-engined buses with the Routemaster, and had developed a rear-engined version of the RM itself. This vehicle, the FRM, was most regrettably costed out of the market following the formation of British Leyland in 1968, before the prospect of double-deck OMO became a reality.

Following the trials and bearing in mind vehicle availabilities, the DMS class of Daimler Fleetline with angular Park Royal and Metro-Cammell bodywork was ordered and delivered between 1970 and 1978 for one-man operation. When ordered, it was intended that these buses should work alongside the MB and SM families and oust crew operation by the middle of the decade. Such was the situation at the start of the 1970s.

Right from the start, mechanical problems had beset the new generation of single-deckers, which from the first day of operation of the Wood Green scheme in September 1968 gave the Merlins an unenviable reputation for unreliability which culminated in two MBs, country MB101 and central MB114, being burnt out in service within days of each other in September 1970. Even when the Swifts entered service, they proved little better, because the shorter body length allowed less room for the engine. This in turn meant that a smaller engine had to be used in an uprated form, leading to more frequent failures.

The original batch of 14 Merlins remaining with LT became due for recertification in 1973, so MBS4 was taken into Aldenham for a pilot overhaul in May 1972 to investigate whether vehicle reliability could be improved. The outcome of this was that satisfactory improvements would prove so costly as to make it uneconomical, even taking into account the disproportionately high cost of a pilot overhaul. So the decision was taken to abandon overhauling the class and to dispose of the vehicles as certificates of fitness expired. The removal of 555 one-man vehicles from the fleet naturally meant that LT was faced with a further delay to the programme of converting services to OMO. This came virtually to a halt whilst DMSs that had once been earmarked to replace some of the last RTs were diverted to replace the RT's originally-intended replacements!

RT overhauls had ceased in 1970 because it was still expected at that time that despite vehicle delivery delays all RTs would be withdrawn by 1974. To this end, the disposal of redundant RTs was rapid until 1972. By this time, however, the failure rate was much higher than anticipated, both for Routemasters and for more recent vehicles, and RTs were recertified and put back into service wherever possible. London Country Bus Services, even more determined to eliminate crew operation than LT, following an NBC directive, had taken delivery of several hundred new one-man vehicles in 1971/72 and thus had many RTs surplus to requirements. To ease its problems LT repurchased 34 of these with the intention of using them as cover for more modern vehicles until the shortage of spares eased. However, in the event two of these RTs, 3251 and 3254, lasted right to the very end of LT RT operation in 1979!

Despite their considerable age, the RTs retained their outstanding reputation for reliability, mostly because they were less complex than the RM and DM families and appeared in many locations from which they had been removed years before, and it was this that helped LT through the days in the middle of the decade when buses were in extremely short supply. It was therefore not until April 1979 that the last dozen RTs took their final distinguished bow from passenger service with London Transport.

In due course the Swift family also became due for overhaul and recertification. Pilot overhauls were carried out on members of three batches of vehicles between 1974 and 1976, and the go-ahead was given to overhaul vehicles of this type. However a change of policy soon occurred and, just as had been the case with the Merlins, it was decided to withdraw and replace the SM family as soon as practicable. Over-

hauling therefore ceased after only 24 vehicles had been completed. As replacements were not likely to be available until long after they would be required, large numbers of SMs and SMSs, (but none of the SMD derivative — of which more later), were given light overhauls either at Aldenham or at garages, and were recertificated.

The Routemaster fleet began the 1970s with its newest members under two years old, but with plans in existence to eliminate the entire class by the middle of the decade. It was soon evident that the disappearance of the class would not be so early as that due to vehicle unreliability among newer types, but it was still expected to make a start on withdrawal in the middle of the decade. Therefore, it was decided to give a number of RMs only a light overhaul and short-term recertification as opposed to a full overhaul, and that these would then be amongst the first to go. By the time that some 60 had been so treated it was evident that withdrawals would not commence until much, much later than intended and the programme was halted. All these vehicles have since received full overhauls in the normal cycle. Withdrawals have so far been limited to the victims of fire mostly by vandals, and to a serious accident casualty, and fourth cycle of overhauls was started late in 1979.

The DMS family was introduced in 1970, intended as the future standard double-deck one-man operated bus, and as part of its publicity for the new type of vehicle, LT christened it 'The Londoner' in the hope of popularising the type and the concept of one-man operation. The staff were not so kind, and amongst other things, called them 'Jumbos'. Because no vehicles were built before the first production batch, as had been the case with the RT and RM, and because the XF was a 72 seat crew bus with a Gardner 6LX engine whilst the DMS was to be an 89 passenger vehicle with a Gardner 6LXB engine, one DMS was allocated for research and development, but the results of the tests were not received early enough to prevent a similar series of reliability problems to those which had affected the Merlins and Swifts. However, this time, the problems coincided with a nationwide serious shortage of spare parts and large numbers of Fleetlines found themselves parked off service. Some regrettably, never recovered and were eventually sold for scrap after five years in store.

With delivery in bulk, it was found necessary to introduce variations in build. Park Royal and Metro-Cammell supplied the bodies, which were not fully compatible as far as spares were concerned. All early deliveries had Gardner engines but these were soon in short supply and Leyland units were needed. However, the Leyland engine did not at first meet new, more stringent noise level requirements as the Gardner had

Upon Westminster Bridge. London's Metropolitans have not proved satisfactory and are to be sold on expiry of their initial Certificates of Fitness. MD96 is seen against a background of County Hall in September 1978.

MCW's development of the Metropolitan is the Metrobus, and large orders are currently on delivery to London. M11 is seen at Hounslow in April 1979.

Leyland's Titan also features prominently in London's orders for the 1980s, and T27 is seen at Romford Station.

done from the start. Eventually, noise levels were reduced, but for the final delivery of 400 vehicles, a fully enclosed engine compartment was introduced to reduce the noise level still further. This had unfortunate effects on the cooling of the engine, and lessened the reliability of the type still further.

After its less than happy experiences with early Fleetlines, LT began to look for other buses to succeed the DMS. Metro-Cammell, the Birmingham coachbuilder constructing part of the DMS order, was at that time looking for a way into the market for complete buses. To do this, they had formed a working alliance with the Swedish builder, Scania, by which Metro-Cammell built a complete bus using Scania running parts. LT had tried a single-deck prototype in 1970, and then ordered a batch of six for comparative trials with Leyland Nationals, and then inspected a double-deck vehicle, marketed as the Metropolitan, at the end of 1973. Further trials followed and LT placed an order for 164 vehicles of this type in August 1974. They included a 'Quiet Bus' engine compartment producing a generally very quiet vehicle. In quality of ride they were a vast improvement over the DMS, and they have proved very speedy buses, but they also have suffered from engineering difficulties, and have lately proved even less reliable than the Fleetline — a great pity as they are fine vehicles. A number of accident victims are already withdrawn and stored derelict and cannibalised.

Other operators in Britain, however, had found the Metropolitan a fairly successful vehicle, and thus encouraged, Metro-Cammell decided to develop an all-British bus. To this end, it updated the bodywork and based it on a Metro-Cammell built underframe and integrated it with the body. Engine is to the customer's choice, but is usually the reliable Gardner 6LXB, mounted in a silent pack. London Transport decided to order a preliminary batch of five for trials with a British Leyland development then known as the B15 and later given the type name 'Titan' which was intended as a replacement for the Fleetline, Bristol VR and even the Atlantean.

London Transport, having decided to cease purchasing the Fleetline, still needed new double-deckers for fleet replacement at the rate of about 450 a year. Rather than risk everything on one type, as had been the case with the Fleetline, 200 Metrobuses and 250 Titans were ordered in 1977 for 1978/9 delivery. The initial order of five Metrobuses (M class) began operating as crew buses from Cricklewood whilst the production batch was fitted for OMO from new, and in 1979 gradually took over from DMS's at Fulwell, Norbiton and Southall garages. At the time of writing, the vehicles appear to be somewhat more successful than the Fleetlines. The Titans (T class) however,

entered service from Hornchurch on OMO services, but have suffered considerably from teething troubles. In addition to this, delivery has only been at half the rate of that of the Metrobus, mainly through industrial troubles at Park Royal Vehicles which culminated in the decision taken late in 1979 by Leyland Vehicles to close the works completely, throwing considerable doubt on the future of the type. For 1979/80 delivery, LT had ordered a further 200 Metrobuses and 250 Titans, but closure of the Park Royal works has had the effect of cancelling the Titan part of the order. The Metrobus order was increased by 100 vehicles to part-compensate.

As regards the single-deck fleet, once the lack of success of the Merlin and Swift families had been recognised, it was to be expected that as many routes as possible would revert to double-deck operation, leaving only those routes which had to be single-deck for physical reasons, or which carried such a small volume of traffic as to require only a small vehicle. In order to investigate the modern single-deck vehicle market, LT studied the four main types of vehicle available.

As mentioned above, a Metro-Scania prototype had been tried during 1970, and a batch of six MSs was ordered in 1972 for comparative trials alongside six Leyland Nationals (LS class) on route S2. Delivery took place in 1973, but MS4 disgraced itself on its first day by running out of control into Clapton Pond. Not to be outdone, LS3 suffered accident damage in its early days, also at Clapton Pond. London Transport decided not to continue with the Metro-Scania experiment, and the class was to be put to store in 1976, five being sold to Newport Corporation in 1978, where they operate alongside a large fleet of similar vehicles. The survivor had been destined for experimental use but was awaiting disposal late in 1979.

The Leyland Nationals were not entirely successful either, but in 1975, LT took up the offer of an early delivery of 51 vehicles of an updated specification to form a fleet of spare buses to compensate for the large number of Swifts out of service. These proved more reliable than earlier examples, and LT ordered further batches of 50 in 1976 and 160 in 1977 to replace further Swifts. These have proved very reliable in service and accordingly, further orders of 30 and 140 have now been delivered providing the unusual modern-day phenomenon of speedy delivery of a relatively reliable bus! Eventually, these will be used to replace, directly or indirectly, all remaining Swifts.

The RF (AEC Regal IV) since 1953 had been the standard central area single-decker and as such had led a quiet life very competently, but by the mid-1970s it was felt that the time had come to seek replacements for those survivors which had been converted to OMO

The famous London RF class reached the end of its 27-year life in 1979. RF381 is shown at Walton-on-Thames in March 1979, nearing the end of its days.

AEC Merlin MBA541 underwent its first full overhaul at the age of 10 in 1979, after the type had finally been adjudged suitable for its work. It is seen at Waterloo Station in April 1979.

The two-door Leyland National is LT's latest standard single-deck model, and has proved satisfactory in London use. LS10, a 1976 delivery, at Hounslow in April 1979.

during the 1960s and 1970s. Accordingly, a Bristol LH was inspected in 1973, and, being found suitable, an order for 95 was placed late in 1974 and the buses were delivered in 1976/7. Because of service cuts and conversions to double-deck fewer LHs were ordered than RFs remaining, but the last two RF routes were converted to LS operation. The end for the fine, reliable, but now veteran vehicles came at the end of March 1979.

In 1971 the GLC decided to sponsor a series of local bus services in areas of the capital with only a low traffic potential. Accordingly LT was asked to operate these routes and acquired a fleet of 16 Ford Transit minibuses with Strachans bodywork which became the FS class in 1972. The four routes, B1, C11, P4 and W9, were successful enough to warrant retention after their six-month trial period was over, and the C11 was so well used as to warrant the allocation of an extra bus. Another FS was ordered and a further three were also delivered in 1973 for the operation of a Dial-a-Bus service in Hampstead Garden Suburb. This also proved successful and yet another extra vehicle was ordered, this time with a Dormobile body as Strachans was no longer in business. Dial-a-Bus was later replaced by a fixed-route service, H2, using the same vehicles.

Traffic on the C11 still grew, and it became evident that larger vehicles were required. A batch of six Bristol LHSs was delivered in 1975 for the C11, to be followed by a further 11 for the other three original services in 1977. FSs remain on route H2, and on similar service PB1, which commenced at Potters Bar in 1977, neither of which can physically take larger buses. As the Transit is a lightly-constructed bus, a batch of five further FSs was ordered for their replacement during 1978, arriving in 1979.

London Transport has, during the second half of the decade, taken into stock a number of second-hand vehicles. This process started in 1975 when 13 Routemaster coaches were made redundant from the British Airways London to Heathrow Airport service. Because of the shortage of buses LT acquired these and put them to work on route 175. After a year or so, following complaints from staff about the lack of grab-rails, they were taken out of passenger traffic and three were converted to training vehicles, the remainder being used as staff buses, replacing time-expired RTs. A further 14 were taken into LT stock in 1976 and the remaining 38 were acquired in 1979 following the withdrawal of the British Airways service. These also entered service as staff buses.

In 1975-77, seven former Midland Red D9 buses were operated by Obsolete Fleet Ltd on LTs behalf on the Round London Sightseeing tour. The Midland Red equivalent of the Routemaster, they were converted to open-top for use on the tour as the OM class. To replace these, LT itself acquired seven of Bournemouth Corporation's fleet of ten convertible open-top Daimler Fleetlines dating from 1965. These were modernised and repainted into LT livery as the DMO class and operate the tour open-top in the summer, but with roofs on in the winter. The OM's still appear on the tour from time to time as extras.

The most significant acquisition, however, has been of the entire London Country Routemaster fleet except for the prototype, RMC4. These buses started arriving late in 1977, and all had arrived by early in 1980 as and when they could be released by LCBS. Twenty-one of the first batch of 68 to arrive were deemed beyond repair and were sold for scrap, but the remainder are all expected to see further use in London. The RMCs and RCLs are to form the basis of the future training fleet whilst the RMLs are to be overhauled for the passenger fleet, although some are currently trainers. It is possible that at some future date, the RCLs may also enter passenger traffic.

In addition to this, LT is also acquiring a number of Routemasters from Northern General, the only operator other than LT and British Airways to buy these excellent vehicles. A number was sold to various dealers, preservationists and private operators, and some operate on the Sightseeing tour alongside the London Transport FRM.

In December 1979 LT took into stock seven of these vehicles, acquired from E. Brakell of Cheam and two further buses direct from Northern General, numbering them RMF2761-9, and more are to follow. Unlike the two similar buses bought from Northern General in 1978 and broken up for spares, these are destined for passenger use.

London Transport is always investigating methods of improving the standard of the existing fleet and several vehicles are allocated to Chiswick Works for development purposes. RM8 was allocated to research from new, but following the wrecking by fire of RM1368's upper deck, that vehicle was rebuilt as a single-decker and allocated to research to release RM8 to passenger traffic in 1976. RM1368 is used for various experiments which have in the past included a liquefied petroleum gas engine. RM116 is also in use for the development of an advanced suspension known as Active Ride Control, even though the RM's suspension is already among the best of any type of vehicle. Two-way radios are now fitted to the majority of RMs, both for control and emergency purposes, and taped-music playing equipment was fitted to Shoplinker RMs, FRM1 and the DMO Class.

Among the more modern vehicles, DMS88 underwent sound-deadening experiments and these were followed by trials with DMS854 which led to the

Bristol LH6L/ECW BL95, painted red and yellow, is one of the buses provided by LT for a London Borough of Hillingdon-sponsored service. The bus is seen at Rickmansworth Station in December 1977.

B20 design as applied to the last 400 DMSs. Other experiments with the Fleetlines have included trials with a hydro-static drive transmission system on DM1787 which is still on test, and the fitting to five DMSs of Clayton hydraulic brakes, a system similar to those on one variant of the RM. The Merlins are represented by MBS217 in use for electrical experiments and by MBA458 which was fitted with a Voith automatic transmission and retarder in 1976 — a system which was so successful as to be ordered for future designs of bus as standard.

To meet traffic requirements 104 SMSs were converted to SM configuration and recoded SMD by sealing the centre doors and filling in the step well, removing the automatic fare collection equipment and upseating the bus to 42. They did not last very long as they were withdrawn on expiry of their initial certificates of fitness. One of the requirements laid down for one-man operation by the T&GWU had been the provision of assistance in fare collection by automatic ticket machines. This was provided on MBSs, SMSs, DMSs, Ts and M6 onwards, but was little used in general, and was withdrawn from use in 1979. On Metrobuses, it is to be replaced by a bench seat.

Since the war, London bus livery had been becoming steadily plainer, but during the 1970s, it reached both the most drab and the most colourful for many years. The standard livery degenerated to a plain, all-over red, fortunately then relieved by yellow doors, on the DMS, and, after experiments with DMS46, by a white surround to the upstairs windows. This was continued on to the MDs, Ms and Ts, with a band around the windows on FSs, BLs and BSs, but is now to be discontinued. But throughout the decade the London scene has been enlivened by buses in unusual liveries. Starting with RM1737 in August 1969, many vehicles received distinctive all-over advertising liveries for various companies during the first half of the decade. All were RMs except MBA606 advertising Chappell's Music Store, and this phase ended with the disappearance of RM1676, the English Apples and Pears bus, back into fleet livery in 1976. Uniformity of livery was not regained, however, for trials were already being held with RMs 2 and 442 of a livery to celebrate Her Majesty The Queen's Silver Jubilee. Subsequently 25 Routemasters were outshopped in silver livery, with specially designed carpets fitted, each sponsored by individual advertisers and these ran in service during the summer of 1977 before being repainted into standard colours. RM2, however, was repainted into a prototype livery to celebrate the 150th anniversary of the founding by George Shillibeer in 1829 of the first London bus service. Twelve RMs and a DM operated in this livery during 1979. Further colour was injected into the scene by the repainting of 16 RMs with a broad expanse of yellow to identify buses on the experimental 'Shoplinker' service, withdrawn in September 1979 when the buses were soon repainted into standard livery. Yet more colour, this time in the various shades of green used by London Country, has appeared with the acquisition of that operator's Routemaster fleet. Whilst RML's for service are repainted red, the RMCs and RCLs for training are remaining green for now — only one RCL had been repainted red by October 1979. The British Airways Routemaster fleet also introduced variety — the first thirteen were operated in BA red before repainting to standard, whilst most of the rest have operated in blue and white as staff buses.

A surprise move in December 1979 was the appearance of RM1237 in an all-over advertising livery for Addis, illustrating Wisdom toothbrushes, and bringing a further shade of red to LT liveries!

What of the future? It has steadily been growing more evident that delays caused by and to general traffic in Central London by and on one-man buses are unacceptable. It is now proving so costly to provide extra buses and crews to maintain the former standard of service with one-man buses that crew bus operation may in the long run be more economic. Already route 106 has reverted to two-man operation, and the Routemaster family — the condemned men of 1970 when still relatively new — are now the only vehicles that seem to have a more-or-less guaranteed future — under present policies! Who knows, perhaps they will be even longer lived than the RT, which finally died honourably in 1979 after some 40 years. It appears that dissatisfaction with the standard of reliability of the DM family and the MD will see the end of these classes within a few years, whilst the development of the Titan suffered a severe hiatus in 1979 when Leyland announced the closure of the Park Royal factory to take effect from the middle of 1980. This caused uncertainty about the future of the model, but late in 1979, Leyland announced that the Titan would continue, with the underframes built at the Leyland National plant and incorporated with the bodies at the ECW factory in Lowestoft. As soon as this was announced, LT confirmed that future orders would be split between the Metrobus and the Titan, but a long delay is bound to ensue during the transfer of production to Workington and Lowestoft. The Metrobus looks likely to be a satisfactory successor to the OMO double-deck fleet, but perhaps the ultimate solution will be a bus designed by London Transport itself to meet its own, of necessity, exacting requirements, based on its own successful Routemaster design. A project of this nature (the XRM project) has been under way for some while, and a first prototype may be built early in the 1980s.

A few details of the XRM were announced early in 1980. It will be shorter and lighter than current rear-engined designs, and the engine will be under the staircase. Other features will be a very tight turning

circle with a standard two-axle layout, and a low front step height. A high proportion of the parts will be standard with the existing Routemaster. The first prototype is to be built in 1981 and is to be followed by another before mass production which is projected for the later 1980s.

As regards the single deck fleet, the only survivors of the unfortunate fleet of Merlins and Swifts are the Red Arrows, to which type of work the Merlins appear well-suited as they are now performing reliably, and the few overhauled and recertificated SM and SMS vehicles that remain which are being replaced in the main by Leyland Nationals. London Transport's fleet of these vehicles began in earnest to fill a gap caused by SMS unreliability, but, contrary to their early provincial record, they have generally proved reliable in London use, and may well have an extended life with LT. A replacement batch of FSs was delivered as the only suitable replacement vehicles considering the type of route they are used on, and the BLs are filling the gap left by the withdrawal of the trustworthy RFs quite adequately.

We now look forward to the 1980s with interest. It seems likely that many Routemasters will still be there at the end of the decade — but what will be there with them? Metrobuses? Titans? More Routemasters? We shall see.

The familiar London Routemaster looks set to remain familiar for some years to come. Silver Jubilee bus SRM16 (RM1920) at Trafalgar Square in July 1977.

Above: Two of LT's Metro-Scanias at Clapton Pond in 1973, at the start of their brief (three-year) life in London service.

Below: Even shorter-lived was the operation of ex-British Airways Routemasters in passenger service. RMA10 at Romford in May 1976.

Northumbrian Independence

G. COXON

Above: One of five similar vehicles bought in 1972 by Tyne Valley, of Acomb, providing the backbone of this fleet operating in rural Northumberland. A Bedford YRQ/Plaxton Derwent 45-seater at Hexham.

Facing page: Still in service in 1979, this beautifully kept 1947 Bedford OB with Duple Vista 29-seat body, of Calvary Coaches, of Washington. The oldest vehicle in active service in the north-east, it was providing a summer Sunday service between the Beamish Open Air Museum and the preserved Tanfield Railway.

Left: Hunter's, of Seaton Delaval, operates a daily service between Seaton Delaval and North Shields. This ex-Southdown Leyland Leopard/Marshall 49-seat bus was bought in 1978.

Rochester & Marshall, based at Great Whittington in the heart of rural Northumberland, is now part of the Moor-Dale Group of companies. The fleet provides an essential network of services radiating from the market town of Hexham, as well as Hexham town services. This R&M Bedford YLQ has Plaxton Supreme 45-seat coachwork.

Wilkinson's Coaches of Hebburn, operates a mixed fleet of AEC, Ford and Leyland coaches. This AEC Reliance with Plaxton Supreme body is an older chassis, rebodied.

An immaculate 1966 Bedford VAL70 with Plaxton 53-seat body, owned by Carr's, of New Silksworth.

J. S. Mowbray, of South Moor, Stanley, is one of two partners making up the Diamond group. This Bedford YMT/Willowbrook 55-seater is used on the busy Stanley-Quaking Houses route.

Above: On the former Venture service from Consett to Townfield, a Bedford YMT/Plaxton of Watson's Coaches, Catchgate, leaves the village of Blanchland.

Leyland Leopards with Plaxton and Duple bodies in the smart fleet of The Eden, West Auckland.

Vodka on the Rocks

D. FEREDAY GLENN

It was Sir Winston Churchill who said: 'I have not always been wrong'. Whilst acting as driver-cum-courier and Lord High Everything-Else during the 1979 Vintage Transport Association Holiday Tour of Devon I was reminded, wryly, of those words, for not much — it seemed — was going right! To begin with our annual 'Club' holiday party numbered 13 — an omen if ever there was one! — and it poured with rain all the way from Hampshire to Buckfastleigh, which was to be our headquarters for the week. In the ordinary way a drop of rain would be precious little bother, even with a 30-year old preserved vehicle, but in this instance we were aboard an open-topper and never the twain do mix . . . Having crawled through Wimborne and dawdled at Dorchester, we were subjected to further lengthy delays at the approach to Bridport where even the traffic lights seemed to have gone berserk. The veteran of '49 dragged itself up out of Chideock and assaulted the fearsome westbound ascent through Charmouth but, as I became aware from the gestures of passengers in the lower saloon, all was not well. At a convenient lay-by matters were investigated, revealing a certain grinding noise from the transmission under particular circumstances. Once the A30 was reached at Honiton there was an end to the hill-climbing and all appeared to be in order on passing Exeter by way of the M5 motorway in late afternoon. We reached our destination without more ado, parking the bus beside the Dart Valley Railway's station at Buckfastleigh.

Over Bank Holiday weekends a tradition has grown up for Galas to be held around the railway station. The site is much changed from when it reopened under new management ten years ago because of massive road-improvement schemes for the A38, effectively terminating the former Totnes-Ashburton branch railway at Buckfastleigh. But by dint of much hard work and imaginative landscaping, the new look is becoming quite acceptable. In turn, the Gala encourages visitors and provides an attractive amalgam of road and rail transport alongside each other, with steam exhibits stealing pride of place. The open top bus proved to be the sole upholder of road-orientated public transport on parade on both Sunday and Monday, but one advantage of its being static enabled us to examine the transmission to try and find the unwelcome noise — aided and abetted by a couple of steam engineers! Not entirely sure that the problem had been located, a liberal dose of grease was applied and fingers were firmly crossed for Tuesday's exploit — a trip to Torrington and Bideford, coupled with a visit to Winkleigh on the return journey.

On the basis of alternate wet and fine days, Tuesday promised to be sunny — and so it was. There was a splendid trouble-free run to Exeter, where we glimpsed the Western National Golden Jubilee bus, followed by a most enjoyable ride past Eggesford and Portsmouth Arms before a genuine 1 in 4 hill near Umberleigh. All, in fact, went well until leaving Winkleigh when the dreaded noise returned with a vengeance. By nursing the vehicle along, we got back to

Buckfastleigh and abandoned it under the viaduct carrying the A38 across the Dart, to commence hours of telephone calls seeking help in our trouble. It was some consolation to find useful protection against the elements was afforded by the viaduct overhead, for Wednesday dawned wet. In due course help arrived in the shape of a vast Diamond T wrecker, ably captained by a most knowledgable engineer from Currie's Garage at Chudleigh Knighton, as this was the nearest establishment capable of dealing with vintage buses and their problems. Then occurred the most hair-raising trip in the bus it has ever been my experience to undertake — with brakes disconnected, at the end of a short rigid tow-bar in driving rain. It was quite bad enough following blindly behind the monster on the dual-carriageway A38, but infinitely worse when a diversion entailed use of its single-carriageway predecessor — vehicles roared past without warning or tried to sandwich themselves between the wrecker and the bus, while the sole means of communication between us was by indicators at road junctions. A further difficulty was the need to refrain from one's natural desire to push the brake-

Another of Devon General's six 1972 LHSs, 92 (VOD 92K) in original livery compares with 'Vodka' on the tour, seen on page 35.

pedal through the floor-boards (my previous towing experiences being limited to slack rope or chain).

After what seemed an eternity, this purgatory came to an end without incident and the bus was propelled into Currie's workshop under cover - and that was that! While most other members of our holiday group had wisely 'done their own thing' that day, five of us caught one of the irregular Devon General buses serving the area and alighted at Newton Abbot (still in the wet). With two more full days to go before returning home on Saturday, a germ of an idea came to mind as we wandered around the crowded bus station: why not *hire* a bus for a day's outing? In order to put the practicability of such a thought to the test, we stepped into the local manager's office and broached the matter. I outlined the sort of trip that had been planned for one day's journey across Dartmoor and was pleasantly surprised at the quotation that was given. Of course, it would have to be discussed with the other members of the party first, but . . .

The outcome was agreement to hire a bus from Devon General for our final day, to tour some of the less-frequented roads

and lanes of Dartmoor using the smallest vehicle they could find to suit the purpose. Promptly at ten on Friday morning we were met by a tiny Bristol LHS with 33-seat Marshall bodywork, sprucely cleaned and brightly painted in its National red and white livery. It proved to be the last of a batch of six such vehicles delivered in 1972, rejoicing in the registration VOD 93K — being promptly christened 'Vodka' for its pains — having fleet number 93 to match. The driver was a most obliging chap and, whilst not accustomed to the wilder excesses of omnibus enthusiasts, was quite prepared to accommodate our wishes for the tour.

As if to complete our pleasure, the weather turned out fine and warm as we set off towards Ashburton before leaving the broad, modern highways behind in favour of typical Devon lanes and Dartmoor gradients. Until only a few years ago the narrow road winding north-westward to Dartmeet and Two Bridges was known as the A384 but, wisely, it has since been down-graded and renumbered B3357; with a maximum width of 7ft 6in available to traffic and some severe right-angle bends and hump-backed bridges, it is no fit highway for heavy vehicles of

Representative of a long line of Devon General AEC Regals with Weymann bodies, SR510 in the Market Square at Chagford in 1957.

any kind. As most enthusiasts will know, there are precious few buses and coaches built to the 'narrow' width of 7ft 6in these days, although a limited number were constructed during the 1970s to replace ageing designs from more traditional times. A handful of ever-popular Devon destinations such as Widecombe and Dartmeet were largely responsible for this lingering tradition — as rebuilding a complete countryside in a tourist paradise was unthinkable, it was imperative that some modern designs should be capable of reaching these destinations, however unpalatable the prospect to chassis-maker or body-builder far away in 'normal' parts of Britain! Exactly because of such circumstances were the Marshall-bodied sextet produced, and little 'Vodka' gave a lively account of itself on the almost-continuous 10-mile climb to Two Bridges. No public service exists at present over this route, although an increasing number of private operators may be found joining in the Moorbus syndicate to provide some kind of link with the outside world for villages and hamlets nestling on Dartmoor. A Wallace Arnold coach was making its way gingerly down to the bridge at Dartmeet, while first gear was often needed as 93 grappled with a succession of severe uphill grades as steep as 1 in 5.

Without pausing at Two Bridges, we turned north-east on B3212 for a brisk and exhilarating run through Postbridge — with its historic 'clapper' pack-horse bridge from centuries BC - to Moretonhampstead to purchase something for lunch. Once Devon General maintained a small depot there, but buses terminating at Moreton must now use the space reserved in Court Street car park. From this point I must confess to some feelings of nostalgia for the days when AEC Regals operated a once-daily journey to and from Exeter (the old '29') and sturdy Regent double-deckers appeared on the 16 service between Newton Abbot and Okehampton. With modern three-digit route renumbering and mostly 'unisex' vehicles in National colours that are the same from Kent to Cumberland, the case for some nostalgia is not hard to make out! And wasn't our own 'Vodka' one of the last buses to be delivered in traditional Devon General livery back in 1972?

From Moretonhampstead we wended our way through lanes that passed for the main A382 as far as Sandypark, when 93

spun round on its heel and abruptly began to climb a narrow, un-classified by-way with a succession of sharp corners until stopped short by the looming bulk of the normal 'service bus'. After an amusing dialogue between the drivers, we were allowed right of passage and plodded on to Drogo Castle for a picnic lunch.

Suitably refreshed, everyone clambered back on board for the mile or so to Drewsteignton — a picture-postcard village with one pub, one shop, a handful of thatched cottages and a vast 13th century church. Under its benign tower we joined the villagers for a 'quiet half', while our driver sipped a tomato juice and enjoyed a generous Ploughman's lunch. After pointing out the way to Fingle Bridge, most of our party walked down through the meadows while the bus

Top: Devon General Albion Nimbus 843 takes the curve southwards to Sandy Park on a winter day in 1970 on the short-lived route 22 from Drewsteignton to Newton Abbot via Chagford.

Above: Two ex-Grey Cars 7ft 6in wide AEC Reliance/ Harringtons in the Greenslades fleet, seen at Fingle Bridge in 1975.

followed later on a tortuous descent by grass-grown lane to that well-loved beauty-spot hidden in the Teign Gorge. The little bus turned in the spot provided close by the mellow stone structure and parked where a solitary National coach (with 7ft 6in Plaxton bodywork) had lately stood.

There was time to wander along the river bank, bask in the sun or enjoy a tempting cream tea before the last stage of our Dartmoor excursion — the driver remarked cheerfully that 93 was the pick of the bunch, as well he might after such a performance! With everyone accounted for, we set off back along the narrow way but forked right at the foot of the incline to take a most rural route past farms and under low trees towards Dunsford. Creeping along at a very careful pace, we suddenly came face to face with a car . . . The lady's astonishment at the sight of a real bus (albeit small) in such a spot caused much ribald mirth, but our intrepid transport enthusiasts were content to wait until she had extricated herself and allowed us to proceed.

There was a brief pilgrimage to see the old open-topper when passing Chudleigh Knighton, but it was safely tucked up in its shed awaiting attention to a white-metal bearing, so we pressed on back to Buckfastleigh. The outing ended with a glorious gallop along the A38, the Bristol's gait at speed being surprisingly quiet and restful after all the low-gear

work earlier. A round of applause for our driver, a souvenir photograph in Buckfastleigh and the day was done. But it will be many a long day before ViTA's members forget their 1979 Devon holiday and the exploits of 'Vodka' over Dartmoor's rocky roads! A happy postscript to the trip was chalked-up a couple of weeks later, when repairs at Currie's Garage were completed — motorists using the coastal road may have been slightly amused to see an aged open-top vehicle bustling along one Saturday afternoon in June, but it was a rejuvenated machine heading home to Hampshire and the comparative peace of local Rallies. I've wondered ever since whether someone mingled a drop of vodka with the Derv . . .

Top: Dunsford Village with AEC Reliance 43 on Exeter-Chagford service 19.

Above: 'Vodka' pauses amid unspoiled woodlands near Drewsteignton during the tour, in June 1979.

Stealing that Extra Bow

Do Commercial Motor Shows reflect the market, or do they set out to shape it? GAVIN BOOTH looks at the Shows between 1971 and 1979, a period of dramatic change.

Commercial Motor Shows can be very enjoyable. Part of the enjoyment comes from trying to guess just what the manufacturers will have on display, because selling buses is not really the name of the game. These Shows are the industry's shop-window; prestige displays of their wares for the public and the bus operators.

You can be fairly sure that local pride will have something to do with the buses on display on the coachbuilders' stands. Roe, based in Leeds, always had a Leeds Corporation bus, and now show a bus representing West Yorkshire PTE, its present-day counterpart; Metro-Cammell, of Birmingham, show West Midlands PTE buses for the same reason; Northern Counties, of Wigan, show Greater Manchester PTE buses, and, in the days when it was a separate concern, Lancashire United buses; Park Royal, now sadly missed, showed a London Transport bus where possible; the Blackburn-based East

Lancashire Coachbuilders have never exhibited — without any apparent effect on sales, it should be added; while Alexander, based in Falkirk, usually contrived to have an Edinburgh or Glasgow bus on its stand — but nowadays the company's exhibit is more likely to be an exotic confection for one of the Hong Kong operators.

What is shown at Commercial Motor Shows — and, just as interesting, what is *not* shown — can be a fascinating study. In *Buses Annual 1972* I looked at the vehicles exhibited at Earls Court and Kelvin Hall Shows from 1948 to 1970; since then there have been a further nine Shows, and some amazing developments in the manufacturing industry, few of which could honestly have been anticipated in 1970.

At the time that young and rather ungainly giant, British Leyland, was still finding its corporate feet. Its problems were mainly on the private car side where it was trying to weld a mixed bunch of models into a competitive range; more than a decade later BL Cars was still suffering from the traumas of these early days.

On the bus side things were rather different in 1970. As British Leyland now controlled AEC, Albion,

Left: Motor Show Razzamatazz, Willowbrook-style. Bunnies brought in to help launch the Spacecar coach body in Playboy Club livery.

Above: Equally attractive bodily, though in a different way, the exterior of the Playboy Spacecar, in black livery, on Bedford YRT chassis.

Daimler, Guy and Leyland, there was really no other major manufacturer to compete with at the heavy end of the market. Any competition existed *within* BLMC — model ranges which overlapped to such an extent that something had to go. What happened was that front-engined double-deckers were phased out in 1968/69 — the end of the AEC Regent, Daimler CVG6, Guy Arab and Leyland Titan. The three rear-engined models were allowed to overlap; the Bus Grant scheme was coming into operation, and the first four PTEs were getting themselves organised — so the Bristol VR, Daimler Fleetline and Leyland Atlantean were produced concurrently to meet the demand.

Leyland's single-deck range was about to undergo major surgery. The Leyland National had been introduced to the world at Earls Court in 1970, and production finally got under way in 1972. The massive investment in the National meant that Leyland's inheritance of rear-engined chassis — the AEC Swift, Bristol RE, Daimler Roadliner and Leyland Panther — would have to be pruned. And sooner or later they were.

Leyland's other main single-deck models, the AEC Reliance, Bristol LH and Leyland Leopard, were all allowed to continue, for each catered for a particular segment of the market.

There was *some* competition, of course. The Leyland National had rivals in the shape of the Seddon RU and the Anglo-Swedish Metro-Scania. And Bedford and Ford were moving gradually up-market, with steadily improving chassis which took these manufacturers into the middle-weight category.

But the double-deck market was all Leyland's — for the time being, at least.

The 1971 Scottish Motor Show had the usual commercial section, and the usual handful of buses. These were fairly representative of Scottish, if not necessarily British, practice; two Alexander-bodied Atlanteans, one each for Edinburgh and Glasgow Corporations, a lowheight Fleetline/Alexander for the Fife company, and a Seddon RU for AA Motor Services. Leyland, who might have been expected to produce a National, chose to show an Atlantean instead.

The National was well to the fore at Earls Court in 1972, by which time it was in full production. The Commercial Show that year was dominated by single-deckers, and indeed, by European trucks — a sign of the coming battles between the British and continental manufacturers, as Britain moved towards the Common Market.

Volvo already had a share of the UK truck market, and in 1972 introduced two bus chassis directed at

41

The first appearance of the Seddon Midi was at the 1972 Earls Court show. This midi for Selnec PTE was displayed alongside a Lytham St Annes Seddon RU.

British operators. The rear-engined B59 city bus was aimed at the National/Scania market, though its sophistication and price militated against its acceptance in Britain. The underfloor-engined B58, entering the fray to compete with the Leopard and Reliance, has proved more successful — probably the most successful of the imports.

Other notable 1972 single-deck models were home-bred. There was the Seddon Pennine IV Midi bus, retailing complete at £5,170, which was to enjoy a brief popularity. There was the Bedford YRT, big brother of the mid-engined YRQ, which replaced the unique three-axle VAL as the company's 11 metre model. On the coach side there was the debut of the Duple Dominant body, one of the significant designs of the 1970s.

There were double-deckers, of course — most notably the improved AN68 version of Leyland's Atlantean, destined to become the most successful of the 'first generation' rear-engined double-deckers. Otherwise there was the usual mixture — the inevitable Leeds Roe-bodied Fleetline, the inevitable ECW-bodied VR for NBC, the inevitable SELNEC Northern Counties Fleetline.

But the double-deck status quo was about to be disturbed, and it was known that Metro-Scania, Volvo and Leyland were all working on new models. There was support in some quarters for the Swedish models, which were seen as useful sticks with which to beat Leyland, partly because of poor deliveries and partly because of Leyland's monopoly position.

The biennial Scottish Motor Show is rarely used for important product launches; these, understandably, are normally saved for the London Show. But 1973 was different, and three significant new models were first shown at Kelvin Hall. In the case of the two double-deckers, competitive expediency no doubt dictated the Glasgow debuts, although one did have strong Scottish connections. This was the Ailsa, assembled in Scotland by Ailsa Trucks with a turbocharged Volvo engine mounted at the front — a return to the position favoured by many of the operators who bemoaned Leyland's rear-engine monopoly.

An all-new double-deck model from a new manufacturer was important enough, but the Ailsa was not the only new decker to appear in 1973. The Metropolitan, rear-engined like its single-deck precursor the Metro-Scania, was a further fruit of the union between the British builders Metro-Cammell and Swedish truck and bus builders Scania; although this was the first public showing of the Metropolitan, over

200 had reputedly been ordered from the drawing-board. The prototype Ailsa was the unquestionable Star of the Show, although this was partly caused by the absence of the Metropolitan from the Hall itself — it was shown only in the Demonstration Park. Also in the Demonstration Park was the third new model, the prototype Seddon Pennine VII, the heavyweight single-deck chassis, with Gardner 6HLXB engine mounted under the floor, developed in conjunction with the Scottish Bus Group as an alternative to Leyland's Leopard. The Bus Group was still cool towards the National, and perhaps it was partly with SBG's requirements in mind that Leyland showed a flat-floor dual-purpose version, the Suburban Express, on its stand.

After all this activity there was little that was really new at the 1974 London Show, but there was evidence of steady and constant development. Noise — or the lack of it — was one of Leyland's main selling points, with quiet versions of the Fleetline, National and VRT. In the case of the VRT the sound-deadening was just one of the improvements introduced with the VRT/SL3, emphasising Leyland's intention to continue producing the VRT after the demise of its longer-established Atlantean and Fleetline stablemates.

All the other double-deck models were well represented — including the usual London Fleetline and Manchester and West Yorkshire Atlanteans, along with production versions of the Metropolitan and Ailsa - now labelled *Volvo* Ailsa, following adoption of the model by its Swedish parent.

Single-deck developments were more concerned with new bodies rather than chassis. There was the neat little Alexander S type midibus, based on the Ford A series, and also from Alexander the prototype T type dual-purpose body; Duple showed its attractive Dominant bus for the first time, and arch-rival Plaxton its new Supreme body, though only in midi-coach form. Willowbrook attracted a lot of attention with its impressive Spacecar body — not least because one of the Bedford YRTs exhibited was in the black livery of the Playboy Club, and was attended by a statuesque bevy of Bunnies.

Otherwise the 1974 Show was notable for the single-deck buses which were *not* there; no AEC Swift, Bristol RE, Metro-Scania or Seddon Midi — an indication of the intentions of the manufacturers, if not always the wishes of the operators.

The theme of Leyland's publicity at the 1975 Glasgow Show was 'The Start of a New Era' — and so it was, for post-Ryder British Leyland was fighting to pull through one of its frequent reshuffles. At the

The 1973 Scottish Show, and the flat floor Suburban Express Leyland National.

The amusing Michelin Omnibus, outside Kelvin Hall, Glasgow, in 1973. Genuine at first glance, it is a modern chassis with replica body.

time of the Show it unveiled the first prototype of its advanced B15 integral double-decker, although it was not shown at Kelvin Hall. Instead Leyland showed another milestone — Glasgow's 1,000th Atlantean; alongside was a National for Grampian Region, one of only a handful of Nationals ordered by Scottish operators at that time.

The only new single-deck chassis of immediate significance were not at the Show either. These were Bedford's YLQ and YMT, bigger-engined successors to the YRQ/YRT range; as commercial vehicles have got bigger, available space at Kelvin Hall seems to have shrunk, with the consequent spawning of 'fringe' dealer's shows, and more recently, overflow displays and continued demands for separate Scottish car and commercial shows. So the YLQ and YMT were to be seen at the SMT show.

The double-deck battle continued at Earls Court in 1976, with two new contestants. The B15 was on show for the first time, and Leyland took the unusual step of displaying a 'used' bus, the prototype which had been loaned to London Transport two months previously, and which had more than 12,500 miles on the clock.

Foden then appeared on the scene with the Foden-NC, in underframe and bodied form. For Foden this was a return to a market it had abandoned

some 20 years earlier, and with a rear-mounted Gardner 6LXB engine, Ferodo retarder and Allison transmission, its new model was in many ways aimed at Fleetline customers.

These were the new models, but there was a good showing of established double-deckers, including a 10.3 metre long 'jumbo' Ailsa — with seats for 107! — for China Motor Bus, of Hong Kong, and a Van Hool-McArdle bodied Leyland Atlantean for South Yorkshire PTE. More traditional deckers included the inevitable London, West Midlands and West Yorkshire Fleetlines, and NBC ECW-bodied VRT — in this case for Lincolnshire. There was also the surprise (shock?) return of the AEC Bridgemaster; the ex-Osborne, ex-demonstrator 80 WMH was displayed on the stand of Road Transport Services, converted with an exposed radiator, shortened top deck and open stairs. In the words of the catalogue, it 'now represents a mid-1920s Omnibus'. Well, hardly.

Single-deck Star of the Show was the new JJL midibus, based on Marshall's Camuter design exercise, and adopted by Bedford, with rear-mounted 330 engine and Allison fully-automatic gearbox. The whole concept was crisp and professional, and attracted much favourable comment.

Otherwise changes in design were largely cosmetic.

Reputedly a 1913 ex-Bristol Tramways Berliet, it seems likely that this bus, exhibited at the 1974 Show, is another replica.

There was Duple's Dominant II, with improved front and rear end styling by Michelotti of Turin, and Plaxton's Viewmaster, a rather uneasy high-floor version of the Supreme, in an attempt to match the high-floor coaches produced by continental builders.

By the 1977 Scottish Show we knew that the Leyland B15 was to enter production as the Titan, and one of the prototypes was at Kelvin Hall disguised as a Greater Glasgow PTE vehicle. The Show had a strong West of Scotland flavour — indeed a Paisley flavour — for the other three buses on display were for operation in that area. There was a Leyland National for McGill, Barrhead, a Glasgow-style Atlantean for Graham, Paisley, and a Western SMT Ailsa, one of ten allocated to Paisley depot.

Lightweight coaches returned to Kelvin Hall with a Duple-bodied version of the new tilt-engined Ford R1114, and a notable vehicle in the Demonstration Park was a Dennis Dominator, representing the Guildford firm's return to the double-deck market.

The 1976 Commercial Show at Earls Court was destined to be the last, for the SMMT had decided to stage a joint car and commercial Show at the National Exhibition Centre, near Birmingham, in October 1978. There is no doubt that NEC is an excellent complex, but the chaos which attended the 1978 Show only served to underline its shortcomings.

More than 900,000 people crammed into NEC during the Show, and there was none of the protection offered to serious buyers by the higher-price trade days which had been a feature of Earls Court. Strong protests from the industry, and demands for separate car and commercial Shows, fell on apparently deaf ears, and it was subsequently announced that the 1978 pattern would set the style for the 1980s.

The overcrowding was most unfortunate, for there was a lot to see. If anything buses for Hong Kong dominated the Show, with three 'jumbo'-size double-deckers for China Motor Bus — on Volvo Ailsa, Dennis Dominator and MCW Metrobus — and a Leyland Victory for Kowloon Motor Bus.

The Metrobus was MCW's successor to the Metropolitan, offering a high degree of sophistication, Voith transmission with integral retarder and a choice of Gardner or Rolls-Royce engines. Its direct rival was the Leyland Titan, appearing in production form for London Transport and Greater Manchester. One step down among the 'new generation' deckers were the Dennis Dominator and Foden-NC. The Dennis was there in force, including a single-deck version, but no Foden was to be seen. There were also Atlanteans and a Fleetline and VR, perhaps — we thought then — for

45

The neat lines of the Bedford JJL, showing the rear-mounted engine, at the 1978 NEC show.

the last time.

Much else was new. There was the Leyland National 2, with bigger engine, although subsequent events have overtaken that launch, and the 'real' National 2, with front-mounted radiator, did not appear until 1979. The 1978 Show bus was, in effect, a National 1½.

Then there was the Leyland/DAB articulated chassis, and the appearance on car park shuttle duties of the MAN 'Bendibus' — evidence of the British interest in artics, and in particular South Yorkshire PTE's orders.

MCW had its new underfloor SM chassis on display, and Bedford had a JJL — again in pre-production form. Tricentrol showed a shortened (9 metre) Ford R1014 chassis, a result of the revival of interest in midi-length coaches.

Plaxton launched its face-lifted Supreme IV range, while Moseley/Caetano and Van Hool also had new models to display. Duple chose not to exhibit at Birmingham.

Kelvin Hall in 1979 had a poor showing of buses. There was a 'real' National 2, in the colours of Highland Omnibuses, an Alexander-bodied lowheight MCW Metrobus for Alexanders (Midland) and a short Ford/Duple coach for Parks of Hamilton. Leyland

had intended to display a production Titan for Greater Glasgow, but the decision to close Park Royal works, and the doubt which then hung over the Titan's future, meant that a ZF gearbox Leopard chassis was substituted, aimed at the market share vacated by the now-discontinued AEC Reliance; the Leopard was displayed alongside a new Cub chassis, representing Leyland's new middle-size Bathgate-built model. A complete Cub, bodied by Wadham Stringer, was available in the Demonstration Park.

I have concentrated mainly on the British-made vehicles in this review of the nine 1970s Shows, but the continentals were increasingly in evidence. Mercedes-Benz had led the way in the 1960s, but the next decade was dominated by the Swedish builders, with Volvo's successful B58, and UK/Swedish liaisons like the Ailsa and Metro-Scanias. More recently MAN and DAF have been around, both at Shows and in British fleets.

On the coachbuilding side there has been the Molesey/Caetano range, imported from Portugal, and Van Hool and Jonckheere from Belgium (and, in the case of Van Hool, from Eire and Spain, too). Pressure from continental builders can only increase, with European manufacturers regularly announcing their intention to enter the UK market. Price has tended to

For the 1977 Scottish Show this prototype Leyland Titan was painted in Greater Glasgow PTE livery.

tip the balance against the continentals, but there is evidence of a growing demand for prestige coaches, and many operators are prepared to pay a premium rate for these.

Price increases have been very much the theme of the 1970s, and it is sobering to consider the leap in normal costs of passenger vehicles over the decade. In just five years between 1973 and 1978, for instance, the cost of a Bedford YRQ/YLQ with a Plaxton coach body had jumped from £11,326 to £25,964; and an 11metre Leopard/Plaxton, selling at just under £10,000 in 1968, cost nearly £40,000 exactly ten years later. And today's double-deckers can easily break the £50,000 barrier — with no end in sight.

So what have we seen at the 1970s Shows? We have seen many new models, both British and, increasingly, continental. We have seen some models, like the Seddon Midi and MCW Metropolitan, come and go.

The double-deck market has been particularly volatile, and with other builders like Scania hovering in the wings, showed no signs of cooling down. The single-deck bus role has largely been assumed by the Leyland National, while Bedford and Ford have continued to battle it out for the 'popular' end of the coach market. With the demise of the AEC Reliance after an amazing 26 years, the Leyland Leopard was increas-

ingly challenged by Volvo in the heavyweight sector, with DAF making steady inroads.

In a fast-changing world, speed is an essential ingredient in selling buses. It is not just a question of fast deliveries — it starts even before then. Operators quickly lose faith if manufacturers display new models at an early stage and then hide them away as development work continues. Certainly this is preferable to untried buses being sold to unsuspecting customers, with all the drama and consequent bad publicity that can involve — but when bus operators go shopping they often look for a tried and tested product, quickly and easily available.

Two 1976 models illustrate the danger of too much delay. Foden's double-decker first appeared at the 1976 Show, and seven prototypes were built. In 1979 the company announced that the bus would be ready for production 'during the next eighteen months' — suggesting 1981 at the earliest, and the best part of five years since its launch. The prototype Bedford JJL midibus also appeared in 1976, and again in 1978, and as I write little is known about its production plans or its price.

With no lack of market choice, and Bus Grant set to be phased out, it is tempting to ask if Foden and Bedford have perhaps missed the bus.

South Wales in the Sixties

A. MOYES

1 Bus hunting in South Wales should presumably begin at Cardiff's Central bus station. Not that Cardiff typifies industrial South Wales, but, thanks to the wide variety of operators found there, most published bus photographs of the area's fleets seem to have been taken at this spot.

Hence, this sequence starts with a July 1962 view of the southernmost stands. Most prominent are a characteristic Cardiff City Transport pair of that period, both with what appear, superficially, like East Lancashire bodies, even to that curious asymmetrical bulkhead window arrangement. The nearer is one of 20 Bristol KW6Gs — a chassis type unique to the city — dating from 1948 and in this case lasting till 1967. The body on 127 (DUH 314) was built by Bruce using East Lancs frames. Bruce's progenitors were the local firm of Air Dispatch, builders of the body on the AEC Regent II to the right. The early postwar years generated many local bodybuilders keen to exploit pent-up demands. Not surprisingly, when Bruce ceased to build bus bodies in the early 1950s, the city chose East Lancs bodywork for its subsequent purchases of Guy Arab, Daimler and AEC dds.

To the rear are representatives of two of the area's large companies: on the left, a Red & White Bristol MW6G in the newly-adopted coach livery. R&W was strongly involved in the express links into the national coaching system, particularly at Cheltenham. To the right, a glimpse of a Western Welsh Park Royal-bodied AEC Regent V, probably bound for Barry. The BET fleets of South Wales contained large proportions of AEC dds, and the Rhondda and Western Welsh ones were frequently seen here.

The city's trolleybuses did not enter the bus station, but only a short distance to the right was the terminal of the rare single-deck trolleys, serving Tiger Bay.

---

2 From Wales' largest to (almost) smallest municipality involved only ten miles but a different landscape, beyond the southern rim of the coalfield. Bedwas and Machen are two mining communities near Caerphilly whose Urban District Council began to run buses into the latter in 1922. After the war, the UDC also began to participate in the useful Caerphilly-Machen-Newport route, and in 1968 achieved a share of its major extension 15 miles north along the whole length of the upper Rhymney valley to Rhymney Bridge, joint with Red and White and the Gelligaer municipality.

For many years the fleet had only three vehicles. Double-deckers appeared first in 1947, and a year later, two Albion dds bodied by another homespun, shortlived coachbuilder appeared. These Welsh Metal Industries concoctions looked fearsome and sounded so guttural as to induce acute camera-shake at first sight. Gradually, more normal Massey-bodied AEC Regents infiltrated, though within a maximum fleet size of seven. The last dd fling came in 1968, possibly inspired by neighbour Caerphilly in being — as the picture shows — a Leyland PD3 with what is thought to have been the last side-gangway lowbridge body built, by Massey. PAX 466F is here entering Caerphilly bus station in 1974, in as-new condition except for bearing the fleet number 96 in the newly-created Rhymney Valley District Council's stud.

---

3 Independents mushroomed in South Wales in the 1920s, and some rapidly built up strategic, frequent routes. A little of that flavour is perpetuated by Jones Omnibus Services Ltd, which NBC took over in 1969 but which has somehow maintained its identity and the dubious privilege of being the only fleet in NBC blue. In independent days, Jones provided a flash of cream and blue brightness from Newport to Ebbw Vale, and within even its buses the exhortation that 'Fish and Chips are not allowed in this coach' made for individuality.

Ebbw Vale is one of the former iron-making towns spaced along the northern outcrop of the coalfield. Without the controversial rebuilding of the steelworks in the 1930s it would doubtless have suffered the even more pronounced unemployment of its neighbours Brynmawr, Tredegar and Rhymney. So Ebbw Vale has much more new housing than its neighbours, and this leaks out to the village of Rassau three miles to the north. Edmunds of Rassau has run buses into Ebbw Vale since the 1920s and is more typical of the area's surviving stage independents in running short, frequent urban rather than inter-urban routes.

Although using omo sds such as an ex-Alexander AEC Reliance, Edmunds used dds in earlier years. This ex-Southdown Leyland TD5 with postwar Park Royal body was seen busy at work at Ebbw Vale Palace in 1962; it had replaced an Albion Venturer/Welsh Metal Industries dd bought new, and was in turn replaced by former AEC Bridgemaster demonstrator 9 JML, in Birmingham livery.

3

4 The South Wales coalfield valleys cut deeply into otherwise high, bare plateaux, and contain virtually all of the 19th century ribbons of housing and mining. Eight miles up the Rhymney valley from Caerphilly's impressive but incongruously-placed castle, passing the former Gelligaer municipality's bus depot en route at Hengoed, Bargoed is reached. The Gelligaer livery was a daring green, red and grey, being the colours of the local Labour party which in 1928 decided that their Urban District should run buses. At Bargoed, their mainly sd vehicles met those of another small municipality, the West Monmouthshire Omnibus Board, the joint product of the Bedwellty and Mynyddislwyn UDCs. Its presence in Bargoed was (and still is, under the blander post-1974 title of Islwyn District Council) on the famous route over the hill from the next valley, the Sirhowy, at Markham. In the 1920s, new colliery housing was built on the interfluve, encouraging the newly-established Board to set up a route whose eastern end gave little hint of the fearsome descent into the Rhymney valley, plunging down through Aberbargoed at a maximum of 1 in $4\frac{1}{4}$, corkscrewing beneath the old Brecon & Merthyr Railway's bridge, crossing the river Rhymney into Glamorgan, and then climbing again, into Bargoed. From its inception in 1927 to the time of its diversion

away from the hill in December 1963, special vehicles were needed for the Bargoed-Markham route, and the senior drivers were concentrated on it. The eight rare vehicles bought began with Swiss Saurers (1927), then the choice in the 1930s moved to Leyland (a pair of the Bull lorry chassis, followed by one of the more well-known Beavers). 1949 brought a Foden PVSC6 which initially carried the Dodson body from the first of the Bulls; this was followed two years later by a second Foden which, as the photograph shows, was neatly bodied by Willowbrook. An identical body was used to reclothe the first Foden in 1953. The final 'hill vehicle' appeared in 1959, in the form of the justly-famed shortened Leyland PD2/38 dd chassis UWO 638. Again this was bodied by Willowbrook, like the Fodens with only 31 seats in a chubby body. When the need for special vehicles ceased, the Fodens experienced only rush hour use until scrapping in 1965, while the Titan was, as intended, fitted with a new lowbridge Massey body in 1966. So ended a fascinating bus idiosyncracy, which Islwyn's pale blue omo sds do not match.

5   South Wales has a numerically larger group of independents making a living from works services. With the collapse of the older industries and the patchy location of the new, there has been a steady development of contract services sometimes over long distances.

Moving west from Ebbw Vale through bleak moorland battered by opencast mining one eventually drops through Dowlais to Merthyr Tydfil. Dowlais is redolent of the depression. Confronted by its huge idle ironworks, the then Duke of Windsor was moved to say that 'something must be done'. Little more was done than clear the site, and a corner provides a home for Morlais Motors. This is a large-scale operator of contracts. On this photograph at the Penydarren yard are a couple of consecutively-registered former Southdown coaches rebuilt by Beadle from bits of prewar Leyland TS8s. Their curvaceous lines are somewhat let down by the cardboard boxes stuffed across their radiators and recalling that it was a cold February day in 1964. They flank Morlais No 23, one of three Rowe Hillmasters, which constituted 60% of that builder's output of underfloor-engined chassis. Morlais built the bodies

themselves on Metal Sections frames; the end product was sufficiently angular and basic for operation on opencast sites. Note that Merthyr Borough licensing authority had still not exhausted its original two-letter mark by 1958, testimony to the low ownership of cars in this area.

The Hillmasters were a stable feature of the Morlais fleet whilst quite large batches of second-hand stock came and went frequently.

6   Downhill from Dowlais lies Merthyr Tydfil, down a road on which BET group trams plied from 1901 to 1939. The local authority began bus operation in 1924, and successfully quashed independent opposition (except for Davies' Wheatsheaf Motors) by the 1930s. When this photograph was taken at Pontmorlais depot in April 1960, the fleet was in a fascinating condition.

Occupying pride of place is one of the five rare 1952 Dennis Lance dds with locally-built bodywork by D. J. Davies; this last of the quintet (No 69) was not to last much longer. To its right are a pair of the Davies-bodied Dennis Lancets of similar date which were to pass to Mid Wales Motorways in 1962 and which looked remarkably long for 35-seaters. At its rear lurk two Foden dds with utilitarian Welsh Metal Industries bodies which did little work between 1949 and their going to scrap in 1961. The identifiable one is No 50 (HB 6582). Vestiges of two

other goodies can just be seen: a wartime Bristol K6A utility characteristically given rubber-mounted windows, and on the extreme right, Daimler CWA6 22 (HB 6000). Originally Duple-bodied, it was rebodied in 1955 with a product of the corporation's own workshop on Metal Sections frames. Not surprisingly this could be mistaken for a body by the Belfast builder Harkness, who also used Metsec frames.

Bristols do not appear prominently on the photograph but Merthyr had lots. Readers of *Buses Annual 1971* may recall that many South Wales operators bought this marque, particularly favouring Gardner 6LW engines. At Merthyr, Leylands were perforce bought in the 1950s; D. J. Davies' last efforts appeared on Merthyr Titans in 1955; the Bristol-based coachbuilder Longwell Green was then tried before settling on East Lancs for some noble Leyland PD3s which were only withdrawn in 1979.

7 Merthyr's most audacious route development, to Cardiff, passes *en route* the gateway to the Rhondda, Pontypridd. This UDC was less successful at breaking out of the straitjacket of topography and existing operators than Merthyr. The main traffic axes along the valley floor were covered by its trams from Trehafod and Cilfynydd to Treforest from 1905-8 to 1930-1, and the UDC was only just in time to assert itself as a bus operator before the 1930 Road Traffic Act. So (apart from the route to Caerphilly) its bus routes were mostly short, steep and urban. The Cilfynydd-Treforest tram route was converted to trolleybuses in 1931, which in turn succumbed to buses in 1957.

Outside the trammy depot at Treforest in 1964 are lined up a typical mix of PUDC buses in dark blue and cream, in watery November sunshine. Leading is 1961

Roe-bodied AEC Reliance No 83 — not that one could miss the large, shaded numerals which style survived the adoption of a trendier mid-blue livery in 1971. Behind is one of the 10 Beadle-bodied Bristol K double-deckers bought between 1948-50, whose six-bay construction gave them a very dated appearance which later rubber-mounting of windows only partially dispelled. To its rear, another Bristol/Beadle combination, this time an L5G possibly styled to match the standard Tilling group body then being supplied in quantity to Western/Southern National. No 51 of this group survived the mass displacement of Bristols by AEC Reliance saloons in 1968, as a towing vehicle which remains at Treforest with the post-1974 Taff-Ely District fleet. Finally there is a shapely Guy Arab/Roe sd, unusually for an underfloor-engined chassis having a rear entrance.

8 Doubling back in a north westerly direction takes one to Aberdare, with yet another UDC fleet to see. The link from Pontypridd would be by Red and White, on one of this interesting then-BTC group company's busiest and most profitable routes. Aberdare Motor Services had begun it in 1921, thriving from the railways' requiring through passengers to change at Abercynon. It became a subsidiary of John Watts' expansive Red & White Services in 1927 and was fully incorporated into the main fleet three years later. Not until 1946 did the last independent disappear from this densely-populated 10-mile route. The 12-minute frequency was supplemented by the former Imperial Motors' Swansea-Aberdare-Cardiff service, limited stop and half-hourly over this section.

No less than 57 Leyland Royal Tiger buses were bought in 1951, the Aberdare depot having 21 of them, mainly for the Pontypridd service. Two of these Lydney-bodied machines are at the back of this group, seen in a deluge at Aberdare station in August 1963. The Lydney coachworks was affiliated to Red & White, and after it

ceased in 1951, some of this Royal Tiger order was completed by Bristol Bodybuilding Works (BBW). Leading the group is a Lydney-bodied Leyland PS1, S1649, ie the 16th saloon in the fleet new in 1949, which was to last until 1964. Though R&W lost its identity in 1977 on fusion with Western Welsh, its fleet numbering style has been adopted for the resultant National Welsh fleet. The PS1's Breconshire registration number signifies that it began life with the independent Griffin of Brynmawr. Red & White took a financial interest in Griffin in 1938, so that its stud was not too different from that of its foster-parent when the whole R&W group was sold to the British Transport Commission in 1950.

Group vehicle policy favoured Albion pre-war, though in early postwar years Guys and Leylands were increasingly bought. Standard Bristol/ECW machines had made strong inroads into the fleet by the start of the 1960s, there being 184 Bristols, 125 Leylands, 68 Guys, 15 AECs and only 58 Albions in October 1960. One of these would have been the Duple-bodied CX39 coach which is largely hidden by S1649.

9   Aberdare provided (and still provides, under the Cynon Valley title), a likeable small municipal fleet, and some characterful routes, often up to valley-head villages from which mining had gone. This 1958 Guy Arab dd displays Longwell Green bodywork to good effect, and also the cheery livery adopted in 1960. Contrary to trends elsewhere, this in turn reverted to an unrelieved red in the 1970s.

A fleet of tiny narrow-gauge sd trams of quite continental appearance began the council's transport interests in 1913, with Cedes-Stoll trolleybuses radiating from the spinal tram route along the Dare valley. Trolleys up to Cwmaman were uniquely replaced by trams in 1922, and the others were abandoned without regret in 1925. Bus routes started in 1922 included that out through the countryside to Hirwaun, where Guy 55 (XNY 411) was photographed 41 years later. Some miners' services leak out beyond the old UDC area, west to Aberpergwm and south east to pits in Mountain Ash. Since April 1974 this latter town has lain within the new

Cynon Valley district, but Red & White (or more correctly National Welsh) maintain a fan of local routes there.

Along the main A4059 through Aberdare, dd buses were the norm until 1972, when the fleet became completely omo sd. In the early 1960s, though, there were still a few utility Daimlers and Bristol K6A dds, and no less than 13 standard Bristol/ECW machines — L6As and highbridge K6As. Standard, that is, apart from the slatted wooden seats which were specified for all vehicles until 1958. Deprived of Bristols by the firm's nationalisation, Guys offered a near substitute, variously bodied in Southampton style (Guy/PRV dd), others with Northern Counties half-cab sd bodies using some double-deck parts and hence rather oddly-proportioned, and then the Longwell Green episode in 1958 which realised uf sds as well as the dd type shown here. Some Regent and Regal III/Northern Counties deliveries in 1951 acted as harbingers of the numerous AEC Reliances of the 1960s, though Bristol RESLs reasserted traditional influences in the next decade.

10 The last leg of this South Wales jaunt goes west down the Vale of Neath back towards the coast. Though some way from its centre of gravity, Red & White picked up three large independents in the Swansea-Neath area in 1938 and welded their 130 vehicles into United Welsh Services. Twelve years of R&W group influence led it to have a mainly Albion/Guy/Leyland fleet composition on nationalisation, enriched by survivals from other independents' fleets which also sold out to BTC; thus one could find a Tilling-Stevens/Plaxton coach ex-Richmond, Neath, and ex-Swan Motors' Daimler CVD6/Roberts dds in the United Welsh fleet of about 200 vehicles.

Characteristic of the R&W group were the dd Albion Venturers of 1947/8 whose ECW bodies provided a warning of the group's sale to BTC in 1950. R&W itself had 17 of these, and United Welsh another 8. The latter's 947 is seen here in Cresswell Road, Neath on an April Saturday in 1960. It was to pass next year to McAlpine's Contract Bus Service along with nine newer Venturers with highbridge Metro-Cammell bodies of the type associated with another group member, Cheltenham & District Traction. To provide tangible evidence of the spread of the R&W empire, United Welsh also had five

highbridge Duple-bodied Guy Arabs just like those of Newbury & District; the parent's better-proportioned lowbridge ones were still in evidence until 1968.

In 1960, rarer United Welsh stock was being eliminated fast. Thames Valley was releasing standard Bristol/ECW L6B and LL6B saloons which were to be common on Neath locals until 1966, and Ks, mainly from Brighton and Bristol, wreaked further havoc. As if infected by the pell-mell transformation to Bristol/ECW uniformity, United Welsh's KSW, LD and LS types themselves seemed destined to short lives and disposal — often, ironically, to Thames Valley.

Once NBC had been formed in 1969, the chaotic overlap of routes of BTC (United Welsh) and BET (South Wales Transport) origins in the Neath-Swansea area became even more obvious. By then shorn of its original character, United Welsh was sucked into an enlarged SWT on New Year's Day 1971. Though losing its name, at least its Neath depot was retained in preference to SWT's. Indeed since these photographs were taken, the bus scene in South Wales has changed greatly but retains much variety and interest.

Woollen District

G. H. F. ATKINS

The BET company registered Yorkshire (Woollen District) Electric Traction Ltd in 1901 to operate tramways in the area around Dewsbury. Feeder buses started in 1913, and between 1932 and 1934 buses replaced the trams. Now, under NBC Yorkshire Woollen District Transport Co Ltd, is one of the West Riding Group of Companies. The main photo (*left*) shows 529, one of a batch of 15 Guy Arab IIIs with Northern Coach Builders' 56-seat bodies, bought in 1947. It is seen in 1953 at Huddersfield.

Above: A 1929 Leyland Lion LT1, with 30-seat Brush body, at Huntingdon Street, Nottingham, in 1934. It was one of 17 similar buses.

Right: A later Leyland Lion in Nottingham, a 1934 Roe-bodied LT5A 32-seat bus, seen in 1934.

At Nottingham in August 1937, a new
Yorkshire Woollen Leyland Tiger TS7 with
Roe 32-seat body, one of 13.

Photographed in Nottingham in 1952, a
1938 Leyland TS8 with 1949 Windover
33-seat coach body; it lasted until 1957.

Another 1938 Tiger TS8, seen when new
with its original Duple 30-seat coach body.

Eastern Coach Works bodies were favoured in the late 1930s. This 1939 Leyland Titan TD5 wieh ECW 54-seat body, is seen in Leeds in 1949, the year before it was withdrawn.

New in 1948, this Leyland PD2/1 with Brush 56-seat body is seen in 1949 in Sovereign Street, Leeds.

Originally one of a large influx of new buses delivered in 1948, 599 was a Leyland Tiger PS1 with Brush 34-seat body. It received this MCW Orion 56-seat body in 1954, and lasted until 1967. It is shown at Barnsley bus station in 1954, in drab all-over red 'livery'.

Above: At the Dewsbury depot in 1954, Brush-bodied Leyland Royal Tiger PSU1/13 was one of three similar 42-seat buses delivered in 1951.

Left: Leyland PS2/5 Tiger 697 with Willowbrook 32-seat body, seen when new in 1950 at Scarborough. In 1955 it was lengthened by Willowbrook as a 38-seater, and in 1963 was rebodied as a double-decker by Roe.

Below: An early underfloor-engined coach, a 1951 Leyland Royal Tiger PSU1/15 with Windover 39-seat centre entrance body.

The hard-working Cinderellas of Britain's bus fleets are rarely in the limelight. The first of three photo-features.

The West Midlands PTE Foden tow wagon rights a Fleetline overturned in the icy weather of February 1979.

AEC Matadors have long been popular recovery vehicles, often with uniquely-styled operator-made cabs. This Matador is seen in 1964 with Chesterfield Corporation, with a Crossley-bodied Crossley DD42 in the background.

This East Yorkshire 1948 Leyland Tiger PS1 tow wagon is seen in 1972 at Stirling, rescuing a Leopard coach. The Tiger was withdrawn from bus duties in 1958, and reappeared as a tow wagon the following year, its Brush body somewhat reduced in size.

61

Above: The former BMMO D7 tow wagons were being replaced in 1979 by Midland Red. This D7, formerly a double-deck bus, is at Coventry Pool Meadow in May 1979.

Left: A former Western SMT utility Guy Arab/Weymann, still in use at Kilmarnock in 1972 as a tow wagon.

Below: A former Bournemouth Corporation Guy Arab, rebuilt as a recovery vehicle, towing a disabled Sunbeam/Weymann trolleybus.

It's 1964. Well, it was 1964 when I first visited Aberdeen. There is a line-up of 21-year-old Daimlers — buses which were even older than I was in 1965. All are heavily rebuilt wartime models — my first (and only) encounter with large numbers of wartime Daimlers. They groan into life in suburban Byron Square at the end of the lunch time peak, ready to lurch and bounce their way back down to the city centre.

Now it's 1980. Wartime Daimlers are but a memory. Even Aberdeen Corporation Transport is but a memory. Regionalisation has come along and now the Granite City is served by Grampian Regional Transport. And in these days of a 15 year vehicle life even the buses which were brand new in 1964 have virtually all been withdrawn. Suddenly I feel old. Not ancient, just old. Well, old-ish.

As I write, I gaze wistfully into the distance and stroke my long white beard . . . hey! . . . hold on! (or haud oan, as we Glaswegians are wont to say) . . . I'm not *that* old. Even if I do remember CWA6s, I was still too young to drink in pubs on that first visit to Aberdeen (but not too young to scale the walls of the nurses home with its ridiculous curfew at Foresterhill Hospital — but that's another story; possibly even a more interesting story; but not, alas, a *Buses Annual* story).

So back to buses. Let me regale you with Regal stories. Or tell Titan tales.

If you take a quick trip down Memory Lane and turn right at the end you'll find yourself in Mealmarket Street. This was, in 1964, the terminus for two independents soon to be acquired by Alexanders (Northern) — Burnett of Mintlaw and Simpson of Rosehearty. The Burnett fleet, 14 strong, was entirely AEC in the mid 1960s. The oldest were ex-City of Oxford Regal IIIs and Regent IIIs; between them they accounted for 50% of the fleet. The other 50% were Reliances of varying vintage, including a newish one with Plaxton bus body. Burnett's livery was a colourful combination of maroon, red and cream.

Simpson's 30 buses were a little bit down-market, being mainly and obviously second-hand. In Aberdeen new Bedford and Ford coaches rubbed shoulders, so to speak, with second-hand Royal Tiger buses. In Fraserburgh, the main centre of Simpson activity, things got worse.

Aberdeen Revisited

STEWART J. BROWN takes an informal glance back at Aberdeen as it was in the mid-1960s, with tales of Aberdonians, Leopards, Vikings, Venturers — and a nurses' home.

In these dim and distant days it was very rare — almost unheard of — for a Glasgow Corporation bus to see service with another operator. At the end of their useful working lives — the psv equivalent of three score years and ten — Glasgow buses were fit only for a final trip to the Great Bus Garage In The Sky or, to be more prosaic, scrap. What, you ask, has all this to do with Simpson of Rosehearty? And well you may ask. Simpson actually bought some ageing Glasgow buses for further service. Rosehearty became Valhalla for a fleet of Albion Venturers. (Yes, I know Valkyries would have been more appropriate but when faced with the choice of poetic licence or historical accuracy what can I do?)

These Venturers whined their way around Fraserburgh in the way only Albions can. But, as I found out when I travelled on one, they didn't smell like Glasgow Albions. In Glasgow of an evening you expect a bus to smell of the odd fish supper or two — and very nice too, preferably eaten out of the *Evening Times* (or the *Glasgow Herald* on buses to Kelvinside). In Rosehearty the buses smelt of fresh fish, carried in bulk in boxes under the staircase to judge by the strength of the aroma. After a ride on a Simpson's bus I didn't eat a fish supper for a fortnight.

Simpson had a few other claims to fame — or possibly infame in the eyes of passengers — at this time. They operated the last — and one of the very few — prewar Bristol Ks in Scotland. A singularly bizarre Bristol with its high radiator and six-bay Eastern Coach Works body. They also ran the most northerly RTs, a fleet of which replaced the short-lived Glasgow Albions. The London RTs were in turn replaced by Yorkshire Traction double-deck Leyland Tigers which were taken over by Northern along with one surviving RT. Simpson also owned an elderly Beadle-Leyland rebuild based on prewar Tiger units. Faced with this strange beast Northern numbered it in the famous P class series of prewar Tigers, the last of which had been withdrawn a few years earlier. An ignominious end to a famous class of vehicle.

Burnett and Simpson were taken over within a few weeks of each other in December 1966. However, some 18 months earlier in May 1965 another independent had vanished into the Northern fleet — the grandiosely-titled Strachan's Deeside Omnibus

Service of Ballater.

The title is descriptive. It was run by Strachan. It ran principally from Aberdeen along the valley of the River Dee. The vehicles were indisputably Omnibuses. And, from my brief experience, Strachan's Deeside Omnibuses ran a Service. Reliable, safe, speedy and quaint. Not modern, comfortable or remarkable. But I'm splitting hairs. Taking my courage in both hands (no, I didn't have a carry-out — I said courage, not Courage) I made the journey from Aberdeen to Ballater in a Foden. Strachan's had a large Foden fleet (seven were acquired by Northern) supplemented by three 'modern' buses — a pair of Regal IVs and an early Reliance, not to mention the Regal III and rebodied PS1. These wore a red, cream and black livery.

In 1964 W. Alexander & Sons (Northern), Ltd was but three years old, having been formed in 1961 from the northern area of the original 2,000-bus Alexander fleet. Virtually the entire fleet had been repainted in the new golden yellow livery by the time of my first visit; I saw only two blue buses, both out of service.

The Northern fleet was a Regal fleet, if not a regal one. Everywhere there were 1940s Regals. Not to mention Tigers, and Titans of PD1, PD2, PD3 and PD3A varieties. And a pair of Regent IIIs, lots of Reliances, a few assorted Bedfords and two Albion Lowlanders. The last named were the newest double-deckers in the fleet and were destined to be the last new double-deckers until the arrival of ECW-bodied Fleetlines in 1978, 15 years on. The last independent takeover in the Aberdeen area prior to those in 1965/66 had been Sutherland of Peterhead in 1950. Much of what had been the modern ex-Sutherland fleet survived in 1964.

Northern's was also a smart fleet. Imagine rich golden yellow buses (preferably PS1 Tigers) in rolling green countryside in the early autumn sunlight. There is a slight chill in the air, dew on the grass. Birds sing in the hedgerows, a rabbit hops lazily in the long grass. A photographer waits expectantly for the approaching bus to fill the viewfinder of his camera against an autumnal rural setting. The bus turns off into a narrow country lane which the photographer hadn't noticed 200 yards ahead of him. He swears loudly. The rabbit blushes. Anglers tell tales of the one that got away; anglers and bus enthusiasts have that in common.

Back to Aberdeen, the home of Aberdonians — both human and mechanical in the 1960s. Northern ran a few Albion Aberdonians, a model which was a sort of lightweight Leyland Tiger Cub designed to save pennies — and very aptly named to reflect the legendary trait of the good citizens of Aberdeen (guess who's just been declared *persona non grata* by the Aberdeen Transport Society). Someone at Albions was obviously possessed of a wicked sense of humour. I salute him.

But the greatest difficulty in dealing with Aberdonians is communication. English as spoken by you, dear reader, and as spoken by Aberdonians has little in common. Our language divides us from Aberdonians rather than uniting us. At one stage in my employment (I hesitate to dignify it with the term career) I occasionally found myself speaking to (or at)

The only postwar AEC RTs delivered new to a Scottish operator joined the Aberdeen fleet and had provincial-style Weymann bodies. A similarly-bodied Regent III follows.

One of Aberdeen's large fleet of AEC Swifts
with Alexander bodies of different styles.

Aberdonians on a two-way radio network. They could neither understand me, nor me them. Take an Aberdonian accent, add a bit of radio static and a slow-witted Glaswegian (such modesty) and you have a recipe for an immediate ongoing non-communication situation.

The Corporation — to get back to buses — were still buying open rear platform 'deckers in 1964 — they actually bought their last such vehicles in 1965. These were fine Daimler CVG6s with Alexander bodies. The municipal fleet also boasted earlier Daimlers with Brockhouse and Weymann bodies as well as some which had been rebodied by Alexander. There was also a fair quantity of AECs in the fleet — Regent IIIs and Regent Vs, and even some RTs. These had Weymann bodies and were the only postwar RTs delivered new to a Scottish operator. Single-deckers played a small part; there was a handful of Daimler CVD6s, most of which had been rebodied by the Corporation or by Alexanders.

ACT's livery was green and cream with a grey roof; the grey was discarded from 1964 in favour of cream for the roofs.

In all this variety there was not one rear-engined bus. Conservatism ruled, OK? There was not even a 36ft long bus. All of Northern's Reliances were of the short wheelbase variety. There were only two forward entrance double-deckers in the area — Northern's Lowlanders — at a time when double-deckers with front or forward entrances were quite common in cities further south. (We reckoned in Glasgow that you could always recognise an Aberdonian in a bus queue in the early 1960s — he was the one trying to get into the engine compartment of an Atlantean.)

Time and tide wait for no man. I became old enough to frequent hostelries serving alcoholic liquor. Rear-engined buses arrived in Aberdeen. The first, in 1965, were not exactly the type of buses you associate with rear engines. No beefy 11-litre engines. No fluid transmissions. No wide ultra-low entrance and low floor. Instead, a six-litre engine. A constant mesh gearbox. A three step entrance and a high floor. And only 40 (dual purpose) seats in a 32ft long bus. You've guessed — the Albion Viking had arrived and taken Aberdeen by storm. Well, it had arrived. Forget about the storm — a mild breeze is perhaps more appropriate. They were of course for Northern who eventually built up a fleet of 94 of the beasts, the largest in Scotland.

Aberdeen Corporation bought more conventional rear-engined buses, starting with Daimler Fleetlines in 1966. These were followed by PDR1 Atlanteans in 1967, 33ft Fleetlines in 1971, Leyland-engined Fleetlines in 1973, and since that time AN68 Atlanteans. Between 1968 and 1971 Aberdeen went

A Burnett Reliance being loaded outside the company's Mealmarket Street office in 1964. Marischal College towers over ageing tenements.

This Simpson RT became the only one of its breed to run for Alexanders (Northern) and, indeed, the only four-bay RT to run for a Scottish Bus Group company.

Buses and Bikes/1. A high-speed cyclist passes a Massey-bodied Regent III in Peterhead. It was one of a pair acquired by Alexanders from Sutherland.

Buses and Bikes/2. Some years later a more sedate cyclist (the same one, aged somewhat?) is passed by a Northern (ex-Midland) Fleetline, in Aberdeen.

Semi-detached suburban Aberdeen. A Brush-bodied AEC Regal, originally owned by Sutherland of Peterhead, passes the contemporary Brown-mobile on its way to Northern's Aberdeen depot.

single-deck, building up a fleet of 37 AEC Swifts, the biggest in Scotland.

1965 also saw the arrival of 36ft buses, yet another Northern innovation. These were standard Scottish Bus Group Alexander-bodied Leopards of a type which have roamed virtually every road between John o' Groats and Gretna Green. Ironically, in view of the late arrival of 11metre buses, Aberdeen is the only place in Scotland where you can see short PSU4 Leopards (10 metre) — Grampian run a trio.

The Northern fleet has seen a few changes in the last 15 years. A fair number of the buses acquired from the three independents in the Aberdeen area received the yellow livery, including such unlikely vehicles as ex-City of Oxford AECs, ex-Yorkshire Traction PS1 'deckers, and various Reliances. Sadly, the Fodens and the RT eluded the yellow paintbrush. All of the ex-independent vehicles have now gone.

Odd vehicles were acquired from other SBG companies starting with Western Aberdonians, PD2s and Lowlanders then progressing through Eastern Scottish Reliances, Vikings and London service Leopards; Central Leopards and Fleetlines; Midland Fleetlines; Highland Leopards and Fife Fords — to take just a random selection!

New Fords first appeared in 1971. Followed by more Fords. And more — including some with Duple coach bodies. Finally Fords fell from favour (how's that for unintentional alliteration?) but Duple bodies didn't — and were supplied on Leopard chassis. Leopards with Alexander M-type bodies were purchased when a direct link was introduced to London. For a while Western SMT Bristol REs performed through journeys, operating on hire to Alexanders north of Glasgow — and even displaying the Glasgow to Aberdeen service number. Some also carried Northern fleetnames but retained Western's black and white livery.

Northern was the only SBG company never to operate Bristol Lodekkas — until 1979 that was. Then five were acquired from Midland, one of which introduced the marque, somewhat belatedly, to Aberdeen. These vehicles — which originated from Eastern National — were the first Bristols to wear Northern livery — but not the first to be owned. A trio of dubious LWLs acquired from Mitchell of Luthermuir were operated briefly in 1967/68. But since neither they nor Mitchell served Aberdeen I'll ignore them since they are deemed to be outwith the scope of this article and cannot be considered Aberdeen buses within the terms of reference of the authority bestowed upon me to write the aforementioned article and they should therefore not be mentioned and notwithstanding the brief reference made to them they will be deemed not to have been referred to in any material way. (Regulation 17, article 3, sub-para ii(a) of notes for *Buses Annual* contributors.)

Pause for breath. Restart train of thought which had shuddered to a halt at the buffers in Luthermuir station.

Yes, so in 1979 Northern became the last SBG subsidiary to introduce Lodekkas to its fleet. By this time, of course, the fleetname had become Northern Scottish. It had started as a gold script Northern, changed to a black script after a few years and then changed to a smart black lower case in the late 1960s — a style which survived until the corporate identity Northern Scottish fleetname was introduced in 1978 with its logo of, depending on your view, three triangles, a rectangle with a bit missing, or three-quarters of the Scottish flag.

Buses in strange cities always run to oddly-named places and Aberdeen is no exception. Cairncry and Auchinyell carry hints of ancient Scottish battle cries. Peterculter and Maryculter sound like relatives. Footdee sounds like Fittie. Still there's nothing vaguely obscene like Newcastle's Two Ball Lonen — which leads me nicely back to Grampian Regional Transport which acquired occasional second-hand buses, to wit, Tyne & Wear Atlanteans and Greater Glasgow Daimlers.

GRT introduced itself to the unsuspecting Aberdeen populace in 1975 by substituting a narrow orange between decks band for ACT's broad green area between decks. It also became the first municipal owner of Alexander S type midibuses and something of a pioneer of the Leyland National in Scotland, following the purchase of three by ACT in 1973.

Aberdeen is one of my favourite cities. (I'm now trying to ingratiate myself with the Aberdeen Transport Society.) It is relatively unspoiled. There are few ugly and unsympathetic office blocks to destroy the city centre. No parking meters (!) Civilised buses. And the Foresterhill Hospital nurses home. . .

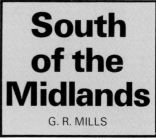

South of the Midlands

G. R. MILLS

A look at some of the independent operators in the South Midlands.

Top: In the fleet of Buckminster, Leighton Buzzard, in 1961 was this ex-East Kent 1948 Leyland Tiger PS1 with Park Royal 32-seat body. It is now preserved.

Left: Charlton Services, Charlton-on-Otmoor, AEC RT (ex-London Transport RT3945) in Gloucester Green, Oxford, in 1970.

An ex-North Western 1955 Leyland Tiger Cub/Weymann 44-seater, in the fleet of Worths Motor Services, Enstone at Oxford in 1969.

New as a demonstrator in 1956, the unique Dennis Pelican eventually passed to Chiltern Queens, of Woodcote and is seen at the Reading Stations bus terminus in 1963. The 44-seat body was built by Duple.

In the fleet of Shurrock, of Brill, an AEC Regal IV with its *second* ECW coach body. It was new in 1951 to Tillings, with an RFW-style ECW body, and received this replacement ECW 39-seat body in 1960. It is shown at Thame in 1969.

Another Worths, Enstone ex-North Western bus, a Bristol K5G of 1938 vintage, with a 1951 Willowbrook 53-seat lowbridge body. At Gloucester Green, Oxford, in 1961.

A 1958 Leyland Tiger Cub PSUC1/2 with Harrington Wayfarer body in the fleet of Charlton Services, Chartlon-on-Otmoor. It came from Gliderways, Smethwick in 1968 and is seen arriving back in its home village after a school contract in 1969.

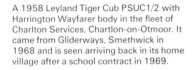

Wesley, Stoke Goldington, operated this ex-Huddersfield utility Daimler in 1961. It was a CWA6 of 1944, with Duple 55-seat lowbridge body.

One of six similar AEC Regent IIIs with Weymann 56-seat bodies purchased by Smith, Reading from City of Oxford. Dating from 1949, it is seen in 1963.

Seen at Kettering on schools duties in 1969, one of a pair of 1956 ex-East Midland Leyland Titan PD2s in the fleet of Shelton-Orsborn, Wollaston. The 59-seat lowbridge Orion body was built by MCW.

This 1950 Daimler CVD6 with 56-seat Roberts was one of five similar vehicles cancelled by Colchester Corporation. Four went to Accrington, and the fifth to Browns Blue, Markfield, and thence to Ronsway, Hemel Hempstead, in whose fleet it is seen in 1963.

Another diverted order — this 1963 AEC/Park Royal Bridgemaster, seen in the Red Rover, Aylesbury fleet in 1969, was intended for Baxter of Airdrie (hence the destination layout), but was delivered to Red Rover following the Baxter take-over by Scottish Omnibuses.

Community Spirit

'In rural areas local bus services have generally been limited in frequency and routing, potential customers being small in number and widely scattered. As a result, the rural lifestyle has rarely involved the frequent use of buses found in large urban areas.' These remarks by Reg Harman in his report 'Rural Public Transport' (published in 1979 by the Centre for the Study of Rural Society) underline the problem that has faced communities from The Lizard to Filey Brigg, and from the Cumbrian coast to the Romney Marshes over the past two decades. Even as early as 1961 the Jack's Report on rural bus services pointed the way with its suggestions for fuel tax rebate and the subsidising of some routes by local authorities. It is as long ago as 7 September 1964 when Lincolnshire County Council led the way by subsidising a new route over The Wolds from Welsdale Bottom into Louth, operated as service 51 by the Lincolnshire Road Car Company (then a subsidiary of the Transport Holding company). By the mid-1970s the vast majority of rural routes were being thus supported by public moneys.

There came a stage in the latter part of the 1970s when even this was not enough to keep services running, and in particular the subsidiaries of the National Bus Company began a continuous process of pruning 'unremunerative' routes. On Saturday 5 July 1975 the Lincolnshire Road Car route 18 between Horncastle and Louth ran for the last time. However, its demise had been anticipated for at least a year beforehand, and a group of local members of the Horncastle and Louth constituency Liberal parties tried out an experimental free bus route along the 18 route on Friday 21 June (a day not worked by Lincolnshire buses), hiring a 29-seat Bedford VAS belonging to Tennyson Tours of Horncastle. Then for several Saturdays in March and April 1975 further trial runs were carried out using a variety of vehicles ranging in size from a BMC minibus up to a Bedford YRT. After a six month interregnum, during which the well-known Lincolnshire independent Applebys took over the route on a temporary licence, the Horncastle Bus Club emerged, as a non-political body with representatives elected from Horncastle, Louth and the villages served by the route connecting those two market towns. The idea was that those who wished to travel regularly on a Wednesday and a Saturday should pay a quarterly subscription, which would entitle them to as many 'free' trips on the route as they wanted. The second source of revenue was to be fares, based on a

DAVID KAYE

Two residents of Gunthorpe, one of the six villages served by the original Eastern Counties Village Bus, prepare to board the Ford Transit for a trip to Holt.

limited stop table, to be paid by occasional passengers. The third means of supporting the service was to come from social events, organised and run by the members. These have included an annual Arts Exhibition at Goulceby, a Country Craft Fayre (with demonstrations by corn dolly makers, weavers, chair caners, etc) at Scamblesby, and a Christmas Folk Dance at West Ashby. The Horncastle Bus Club took over the route on Saturday, 3 January 1976 incidentally increasing the average speed for the complete journey from 19.5mph (Lincolnshire RCC) to 26.8mph, whilst the route mileage had gone up from 17.2 miles to 24.6 miles, by including smaller communities like Fulletby. Regretfully the Club had to apply for a subsidy from Lincolnshire County Council during 1977, after a steep rise in operating costs, and after the six journeys per week had had to be cut back to three.

About the same time that Horncastle Bus Club officials were carrying out surveys of people's needs in The Wolds, in neighbouring Norfolk another group were working on similar lines in the villages that lie off the main road between Holt and Fakenham. However, their solution was a rather different one. The Eastern Counties Omnibus Company (as the NBC representative) laid plans before Norfolk County Council for a community bus service, which would involve the purchase of a small bus and the training of a team of volunteer drivers, together with the regular maintenance of the vehicle by Eastern Counties. The particular type of vehicle selected was a Ford Transit with a 12-seat Deansgate body, in the joint livery of ECOC and Norfolk County Council. This ran until it was damaged in an accident during the terrible wintry conditions early in 1979, when there was up to six feet of snow blocking some of the narrow lanes on the route. It has now been replaced by another Ford Transit/ Deansgate 12-seater, although it had been hoped by the Committee that a larger vehicle might have been forthcoming, since, as I have personally witnessed, it becomes rather crowded on some journeys into Holt.

To obviate this, the latest timetables divide the route into two, so that one journey will serve one group of the 10 villages covered by the scheme, whilst the next travels through the remainder. The bus runs into Holt (where it connects at the former railway station with ECOC

route 768 to Sheringham) on Tuesdays and Fridays, whilst on Thursdays the destination is Fakenham. In addition, demonstrating its true community aspect, on Wednesdays there is a surgery run to the doctors in Melton Constable. There are also school contract journeys from Sharrington and Thornage to Brinton Primary School. For the first four winters the bus had to stand out at a farm at Sharrington, but in 1979 a garage (large enough for a 16-seater) was constructed. As on other community bus schemes, fares are not subject to frequent increases every time diesel goes up in price or the TGWU obtains a rise for its members, so, for example, the North Norfolk fare chart remained unaltered from May 1978 until August 1979, and that of the Horncastle Bus Club from July 1977 until January 1980. It is pleasant to record that Clifford Brown, who has provided so much of the energy behind this particular operation, received the MBE in the 1979 New Years Honours List for his services to rural transport; an award that can be shared by the dozens of others who have laboured, often under great difficulties to bring similar ventures to fruition.

On 6 June 1976 yet another variation came into being in nearby Suffolk. Here the Breckland District Council and Norfolk County Council decided to launch an experimental service from the little village of Wood Rising, via Cranworth, Southburgh, Whinburgh, Garvestone, Reymerston and Hardingham into Norwich on Wednesdays. The independent operator Colin Pegg was hired, and those travelling were allowed 4 hours and 5 minutes to do their

The Holt Community Bus connecting with an Eastern Counties Bristol VRT at the former Holt railway station.

shopping in Norwich. A year later, on 8 July 1977, a second similar service was commenced, using the same tripartite arrangement. This time the route ran on Fridays from Blylaugh, via Billingford, Worthing and Hoe into East Dereham. Both these experimental routes have proved their worth, and were still operating in the summer of 1979.

Sussex has a body with the name of the 'Sussex Rural Community Council for the Promotion of Voluntary Effort in Sussex'; an 18th century sounding title! This group carried out a survey of the needs of the villagers in the sparsely-populated area between Seaford and Hailsham, that had once been served by Southdown Motor Services routes 98 and 198. The organisation established in 1976 consisted of no less than *four* interested parties, namely Sussex Rural Community Council, East Sussex County Council, Southdown Motor Services (as agents of NBC), and elected representatives from the various villages involved. This time two second-hand Ford Transits, with distinctive 15-seat Deansgate bodies were purchased from Eastbourne Corporation, and 'garaged' in the yard at Berwick railway station.

As with the Holt scheme, volunteer drivers were forthcoming from no less than 15 different villages, some of which were not even on the proposed routes. One of the different features of what became known as the Cuckmere Community Bus (with its attractive CCB logo with a wavy line representing the meandering, ox-bow strewn river of that name) was the fare structure, which was described at the time as not so much of a zonal variety, but rather as a 'grid'. On journeys into Hailsham, there was originally a flat fare of 20p, whereas on journeys to Seaford, the 20p fare was in operation for the first six miles, after which a charge of 30p was made. This had to be modified in March 1978, when a more orthodox fare table was brought into force with fares graduated into 10p, 20p, 25p and 30p stages. Whereas the Holt Community Bus supplemented its income by running successful excursions, in 1978 the Cuckmere Community Bus committee started its Summer Sundays 'Ramblerbus'. This consisted of six circular journeys made from May until September, when for 40p travellers could do the circuit joining and leaving and rejoining at any point along a route that actually ran not through, but adjacent to the normal area covered by the weekday buses. A resourceful timetable showed at which stops the passenger could alight to have a pub meal, visit a museum or gain access to the South Downs Way. Indeed the slogan to launch this service was 'Sunday walking can be simple with the Ramblerbus.'

Another departure from the two other schemes examined above was that soon after its commencement certain journeys into Hailsham were extended to the Lion Caravan Site, thus providing a local route for that small town's residents.

Encouraged by these preliminary efforts, the Lilbourne 'Special' went into action in Silver Jubilee week 1977 (10 June to be precise). Serving a group of villages with a combined population of 450, this was started with the joint backing of Northamptonshire County Council and the United Counties Omnibus Company. Running into Rugby from Lilbourne, an unusual feature of this service is that this basic route has bookable connections from Clay Coton, Crick, Winwick and Yelvertoft. In addition on schooldays vacant places can be taken on the contract journeys to Yelvertoft School. The vehicle employed is a Ford Transit from the United Counties Fleet, but this time it has a 12-seat Tricentrol body. During the initial year half the County Council loan for setting up the service was repaid, whilst in the second year quite a surplus was made. Part of this must be due to the fact that 200 private hire trips were undertaken between 1977 and 1979, whilst outings included visits to the Blackpool Illuminations, to go shopping in Birmingham, and to enjoy ice skating.

The Cuckmere Community Bus, an ex-Eastbourne Ford Transit/Deansgate, at Alfriston Cross.

The location of the community bus seems to determine how much revenue comes from that source, for the Aldborough Community Bus in Norfolk in its first year had to regretfully cancel 35 out of 47 advertised excursions. Those planned for 1979 included Cromer Flower Show, Sheringham's Little Theatre, and the Duxford Aircraft Museum (billed as 'A Day out for Father'!). The huge mileage total that driver training takes up is was illustrated by the Aldborough Community Bus. In the first year this totalled 4,090 miles, as against 9,805 miles on scheduled services. Eastern Counties provided a Ford Transit/Tricentrol, financially helped by Norfolk County Council, and this vehicle entered service for the first time on 3 July 1978. As its first annual report states: 'The routes were altered several times during the year as traffic patterns developed of variance with the original survey and passenger loadings and revenue were comparatively light until these timetable adjustments were complete.' Indeed three of the small villages, that were included in the first timetable (Hanworth, Little Barningham and Matlaske) were dropped, and as from January 1979 Banningham joined the network. Again, a standard (or flat) fare was initially tried out with rather high

fares, but this was modified later. Thus the single fare from all the villages into Sheringham on a Tuesday was cut from 35p to 30p. The dreadful winter of 1979 led to fresh difficulties, for although only two operating days were lost, some of the 15 volunteer drivers were snowed in — in one case for three and a half weeks — thus necessitating some drivers having to do twice their normal number of turns. As well as running into Sheringham, on Mondays the destination is Aylsham, on Thursdays Horseshoes (where passengers can transfer on to Eastern Counties route 758 bus for Cromer), and on Tuesdays, Thursdays and Fridays the market town of North Walsham is also served. One interesting community aspect of the Aldborough Community Bus is its use by the Aldborough Play Group for assembling mothers and children for their sessions.

If a prize were to be awarded for the most complicated schedule yet devised for a community bus and for its most varied use, then at the time of writing, this would go to the Bassetlaw Community Bus. The services it offers, together with route maps, fare charts, etc fill a fair size A4 folder, obtainable from Nottinghamshire County Council. For instance on the first, third and fifth

The original Bassetlaw Community Bus, a Ford A, was hired from Leon Motors of Finningley.

Sundays each month it travels between Bircotes and Saxondale Hospital, whereas on the other two Sundays its route takes it from Retford railway station to Rampton Hospital. On weekdays there are two alternative schedules, according to whether it is term time or holiday time. Unlike any of the other services dealt with in this article this one copes with the handicapped as well as ordinary fit passengers. For its first year of operation, starting on 1 May 1978, Leon Motors of Finningley was the hire operator, using a Ford A with a special body, which as well as seating 19 passengers, could take two wheeled chairs at the rear (entrance for the latter being by a rear positioned tail lift). As from 1 May 1979 Lincolnshire Road Car provided an ECW-bodied Bristol LHS6P, which had been specially altered at the Bracebridge Heath works to have its normal complement of 35 bus seats exchanged for 22 coach seats, plus room for invalid chairs accessible by tail lift. Like its predecessor it was painted in the BCB livery of blue and white. Keeping the same livery is vital in maintaining the confidence of some of the more elderly and less confident clientele, as the Horncastle Bus Club discovered when first Keith Lee of East Barkwith (blue/cream) worked their route on behalf of the normal operator, Don Dickinson of Wrangle (dark green/red/cream). It was only when Clifford Brown of the North Norfolk Community Bus threatened (jokingly, of course) that his drivers would lie down in the road rather than drive the new minibus in a new livery that Sir Frederick Wood (then Chairman of NBC) agreed that their old livery could be retained.

1978 also saw the launching of the last of the community buses, which I want to deal with in this article — the Coleridge down in South Devon. Devonshire County Council made a grant of £10,000 to start the venture, and with this cash a 16-seat Ford was purchased, and no less than 24 local residents in the South Hams area were trained to take their psv driving test. In this case the interesting thing is that the list begins with names such as Poppy Baker, Elizabeth Brown, Heather Cummings, Peggy Verniquet and Marcia Widger, for the majority of the drivers are, in fact, ladies. Although it must be pointed out that some of the fair sex do drive in other schemes, and on my tour of the Cuckmere I was driven ably by a vicar's wife. The Coleridge serves 40 square miles of countryside and runs into the

small market town of Kingsbridge, where the local independent Tally Ho Coaches Ltd carries out routine maintenance on the vehicle. A zonal fare structure does operate with the villages participating divided into four zones.

In the May 1979 edition of *Bus* (the house magazine of NBC) was this significant comment on the future of these routes: 'NBC maintains a positive attitude toward the community bus and regards its role as supporting the local network of conventional bus services.' Indeed its chairman on one occasion stated: 'Every village that has a cricket team could operate the service.' However, perhaps the final word could rest with Harry Seal (parish clerk at Lilbourne): 'Use it — don't lose it.' From the way in which local communities have responded to these varied schemes over their first four years, I don't think that there is much chance of that happening, even if it is sometimes difficult to find somebody in a particular village willing to serve on the organising committee. Doubtless the new transport legislation will work towards encouraging further essays into this exciting field of public service.

In conclusion I should like to thank all my many friends in community buses projects all over England, who have assisted me in the preparation of this piece, and especial thanks are due to Alison Abbey (Cuckmere), Clifford Brown (Holt), Ted Edwards (Lilbourne), John Ford (Coleridge), John Hebenton (Aldborough), Mike Newstead (Bassetlaw) and Patrick Reeson (Lincs Road Car).

In May 1979 this specially-adapted Lincolnshire Road Car Bristol LHS took over duty as the Bassetlaw Community Bus.

The unique 1931 Crossley Condor, RV 720, formerly 74 in the Portsmouth Corporation bus fleet, seen in its last days as a tow wagon before it was retired and transferred to the City Museum Department for preservation.

New recovery vehicles are unusual, but Northern General's Stanley garage uses this Ford D, seen towing a Bristol RE/ECW to the Central Works at Bensham.

An increasing number of underfloor-engined buses is appearing suitably converted for recovery purposes. This Crosville Bristol MW6G/ECW became a tow wagon in 1976. Seen in Llandudno Junction depot.

End of the Line

The creation of National Bus Company caused the demise of a number of former BET group fleets. Some of these are recalled by MICHAEL DRYHURST.

The National Bus Company assumed operations in 1969, being a fusion of the Transport Holding Company and the bus-operating interests of the British Electric Traction Group.

British Electric Traction, or BET, had been a tramways builder and operator in the latter part of the last century, and during the years had acquired many bus companies, but by 1968 the board of the company felt that financial success lay in spheres other than bus operation, so that this part of the group's activities were sold, for £35million.

The Transport Holding Company was the nationalised successor to the bus operating side of the British Transport Commission, the basis of the BTC's foundation being the sale of the Thomas Tilling bus group under the 1947 Transport Act. Also, the BTC and subsequently THC, had minority interests in most of the BET group bus companies, via the shares held at one time, by the four main railway companies.

Once the National Bus Company became manifest, it was obvious that some form of rationalisation was both inevitable and necessary, but sadly it has meant the demise of a number of companies, certainly as vehicle operators, because in many instances the company names still exist as licence holders or even as property owners.

A quick trip around England and Wales recalls some of these bus companies.

The main BET operator in north east England was the Northern General Transport Co Ltd, of Gateshead-on-Tyne, and NGT had a number of subsidiary companies.

The last BET tramway operation was by the NGT subsidiary **Gateshead & District**, which was

Left: Albions were for many years standard for Red & White group fleets. This United Welsh Venturer had handsome Weymann bodywork.

Gateshead & District 79, a Leyland Titan PD3/4 delivered in 1958 with an MCW 73-seat body.

incorporated by the Gateshead and District Tramways Act 1880, and initial operation commenced in October 1883, with steam trams. Electric trams replaced the steam cars in 1901 under BET auspices, that body having obtained an interest in the company in 1897, and various extensions took place, but in 1923 a milestone in the company's history was reached when through running into Newcastle over the newly-opened High Level Bridge began on 7 September. Five years later the first tram crossed the new Tyne Bridge immediately after King George V had performed the opening ceremony. Less than half of the Gateshead trams were double-deckers; exceptionally low bridges on the Bensham, Dunston and Low Fell routes necessitated their being worked with high-capacity single-deckers.

In May 1913, Gateshead Tramways inaugurated motorbus operation with a double-decker service between Chester-le-Street and Low Fell, soon after opening another route, to Durham, which necessitated building a garage in Chester-le-Street, and such was the success of these bus services that it was decided to form a subsidiary company to operate them, which would at the same time consolidate the interests of Gateshead & District, Tynemouth & District and the Jarrow & District companies. The subsidiary

company was registered on 29 November 1913, as the Northern General Transport Co Ltd.

By the mid-1930s, much of the tram track and rolling stock of Newcastle Corporation was in need of replacement and so that body had to consider the possibility of heavy capital expenditure on renewals; after an exhaustive examination of the problem, a policy of replacing the trams with trolleybuses was adopted. Allied with the Newcastle Corporation decision was the Gateshead and District Tramways Act 1938, authorising the company to replace their trams with trolleybuses, but the intervention of World War II prevented this, and by the end of the 1940s attitudes and thinking had changed, the motor bus being thought to be a more flexible substitute for the trams, so a Bill was presented in the 1949/50 Session of Parliament repealing that part of the 1938 Act covering trolleybus operation and at the same time extending the powers of the company, to run motor buses, with a change of title to the Gateshead & District Omnibus Co Ltd.

The first conversion was on 5 May 1950, and the last tram ran on 4 August 1951, which also marked the end of BET tram operation (the BET subsidiary South Wales Transport had acquired the Swansea and Mumbles tramway in 1953, which prior to then was a private company). The initial bus fleet was composed of Guy Arab III double-deckers with Brush or Park Royal/Guy bodies, and standard Leyland-bodied PD2 Titans, painted in a brown and cream livery.

Sunderland District Omnibus Co Ltd had beginnings as a tramway when operations by the Sunderland District Electric Tramways commenced in June 1905, from a base at Philadelphia, Co Durham, with routes connecting local villages with railheads. Connection with the Sunderland municipal tramways was made at Grangetown. However, traffic was not as high as expected, the installation of the track and overhead greatly exceeded the original estimates and despite the fact that the company generated its own power, it proved to be more costly than anticipated. A receiver and manager was appointed in 1913, and the company was able to meet its charges, but the growth of bus competition during the 1920s posed a serious threat to the company, to such an extent that it was decided to convert the system from trams to motor buses, this happening in 1924/5, with the change of company title name occurring in 1927. Northern General acquired the share capital in 1931.

Sunderland District buses were painted in a very pleasant blue and white livery, and the blue livery lasted into early NBC days, albeit applied in National style — white relief on blue, with grey wheels. All of the fleet is now in NBC red (or possibly Tyneside yellow).

Tynemouth & District Transport Co Ltd was another BET tramway operator, again initially with steam traction, which commenced in North Shields in 1890, electric trams taking over in 1901. The first bus route was started in 1921, a number being introduced over the next three years including a joint service with United Auto, between Newcastle-upon-Tyne and Whitley Bay. During this time the buses augmented trams on the electric routes and by 1930 were actually running a joint service, so that it came as no surprise when the trams were abandoned, the last running on 21 August 1931. In 1934 the company, together with United, purchased the 'Pride of Blyth' run by a Mr Howe between Blyth and Whitley Bay and another purchase was that of Messrs Hollings in 1950, who had operated local services in Wallsend. After World War II the maroon-liveried Tynemouth fleet standardised on the Guy Arab III with Weymann or Pickering bodies, and after a small batch of Arab IV/Park Royal in 1956, Leylands became the order of the day, with 10 PD3/4 in 1958, followed by Atlanteans from 1959 onwards.

Northern General acquired a controlling interest in the **Tyneside** Tramways and Tramroads Co in 1936. Tyneside had opened a tram route between Newcastle and North Shields in 1902, replacing its trams with buses in 1930. The Tyneside company was one of the smaller NGT units, and its green and cream buses which turned in Newcastle side streets, reminded one more of a well-kept, uniform, independent fleet rather than part of the BET empire.

In September 1927 the North-Shields based **Wakefield's** Motors was incorporated, becoming a NGT subsidiary in 1929. In later years, Wakefield's was operated and managed by the Tynemouth company, in whose maroon livery its buses were painted, being garaged at Tynemouth's Percy Main depot. One of the things which endeared NGT and its subsidiaries to the enthusiast was the fact that vehicles were registered from the subsidiary's base rather than at NGT's head office, and even Northern General had buses registered in Gateshead, Co Durham, South Shields and Northumberland!

The most recently-acquired NGT subsidiary was **Venture** Transport, which dated from 1938 when it evolved out of the merger of Venture Bus Services Ltd and Reed Bros Ltd, both of which dated from the time of World War I. Venture had always been a single-deck fleet, with a proportionately high degree of standardisation, the immediate post-World War II mainstay being CVD6 Daimlers with Willowbrook bodies. During the mid-1950s some two dozen Atkinson Alpha chassis were purchased, followed by 17 Albion Aberdonians, Willowbrook bodying all 41 chassis. After some 15 AEC Reliances, the company standardised on Leyland Leopard chassis and Alexander bodies.

In 1950 the British Transport Commission acquired a trio of north-east operators — ABC Services of Ferryhill, Darlington Triumph Motor Services and Express Motor Services (Durham) Ltd — and merged them into a new company, **Durham District** Services Ltd, control of which was vested in United Automobile Services. A varied fleet was operated, but gradually the standard BTC Bristol/ECW combination took over, and although originally having its own vehicle numbering system, the DDS fleet eventually was numbered in the parent UAS series.

We leave the north-east and move to south Yorkshire. The National Electric Construction Company built tramways in a number of towns, its interests being eventually acquired by BET. In 1902 NEC promoted, and Parliament passed, the Mexborough and Swinton Tramways Act, and three years later the **Mexborough & Swinton** company built a tramway system there, using the Dolter Surface Contact System, but this system was not very efficient and so Mexborough converted to overhead collection in 1908. Routes were in operation between Rawmarsh and the Rotherham boundary and Rotherham and Mexborough via Swinton, with open-top double-deck

Pickering of Wishaw bodied this Guy Arab III of Tynemouth, seen at Whitley Bay.

A Mexborough & Swinton single-deck trolleybus picks up in Mexborough, on the former joint route worked with Rotherham Corporation. The bus was a Sunbeam with 34-seat centre-entrance Brush body.

A Willowbrook-bodied Leyland Tiger Cub operated by County Motors, in Huddersfield.

cars. In 1915 two short, unconnected, trolleybus routes were opened between Manvers Main Colliery and Mexborough and Conisborough and Mexborough, whilst in 1922 the first motor bus route was opened.

In 1928 the two trolleybus routes were physically connected and extended, the last trams running in 1929, when through trolleybus operation to Rotherham took place. Both the motor bus and trolleybus fleets were single-deck, in a pleasant green and cream livery. The first trolleybus conversion was in 1954, when Weymann-bodied Leyland Tiger Cubs took over the Ryecroft route, and the final conversion occurred in March 1961, which also marked the end of electric traction within the BET group, and company trolleybus operation in the UK. Tiger Cub single-deckers were latterly the mainstay of the fleet, although 14 lowbridge Weymann-bodied Atlanteans were in stock. With NBC rationalisation, Mexborough and Swinton disappeared into Yorkshire Traction.

Around Huddersfield are memories of **County Motors** (Lepton) Ltd, which was a small fleet of some 20-odd vehicles that was jointly owned by BET subsidiaries Yorkshire Traction and Yorkshire Woollen and independent West Riding (later to sell-out to the NBC). County Motors operated mainly in the Huddersfield area, in a pleasant blue and cream livery. The company purchased a brace of the ill-fated Guy Wulfrunian, which passed to West Riding, County Motors itself falling under the wing of Yorkshire Traction.

In December 1924, Mr Charles Holdsworth of Halifax opened two bus routes, between Halifax and Brighouse and Halifax and Bingley, operating as Hebble Bus Service. More routes were quickly added and two companies, Briggs of Wilsden, and Calder Services, were acquired in 1928. A year later the company was jointly purchased by the London Midland & Scottish Railway and the London & North Eastern Railway, who concluded an agreement with Halifax Corporation which resulted in the Halifax Joint Omnibus Committee, in which all three parties had an interest, transferring eight routes from Hebble to the Halifax JOC. **Hebble** Motor Services Ltd came into being in February 1932 when BET acquired its interest.

Hebble had a very distinctive fleet in later years because although operating in the region of 80 vehicles, they were always in small batches. AEC and Leyland were the main suppliers, the Daimler Fleetline becoming the company's standard 'decker after manufacture of the AEC Regent ceased.

The 1968 Transport Act, which paved the way for the NBC, incorporated legislation covering the replacement of British Rail members of the three Joint

Omnibus Committees (Halifax, Huddersfield, Sheffield) by nominees of Amalgamated Passenger Transport Ltd, an NBC subsidiary. Huddersfield and Sheffield responded by immediately purchasing the respective NBC holdings in them, but at Halifax the JOC merged with Hebble, the company eventually becoming swallowed by Yorkshire Woollen.

Before leaving the Yorkshire area, mention must be made of **Sheffield United Tours** Ltd, which was a most impressive coach fleet mainly engaged on extended tours and coach cruises. The coaches, virtually 100 per cent AEC, were painted in a smart red and grey livery, and SUT became the main unit of National Travel (East) Ltd.

Another conglomerate with large electric traction interests was the Balfour Beatty Group, which controlled the Midland Counties Electric Supply Co Ltd, which in turn had some subsidiary bus and tram companies, one of which was the Nottinghamshire and Derbyshire Traction Co Ltd. **Notts & Derby** commenced tramway operation in 1913, with a long (15 mile) route twixt Ripley and Nottingham, the Corporation of the latter city entering into a through-running agreement with the Company, which gave N&D access to Nottingham city centre via Corporation track. At Ripley, it was intended that the line would have joined a long, through route from Belper via Alfreton, to Mansfield, where the local trams were operated by an associate company. In 1917 Notts & Derby purchased the Ilkeston Corporation Tramways, a small 3ft 6in gauge system opened in 1903, although N&D was to standard gauge. Under an Act of 1928, the company obtained powers to abandon its trams, and to operate trolleybuses, the first such vehicles appearing in 1932, N&D having replaced the Ilkeston trams with motorbuses in 1931. Notts & Derby's last tram ran in 1933. The trolleybuses were painted in a very pleasant blue and cream livery, the first such deliveries being single-deckers. With the nationalisation of the electricity industry in 1948, ownership of Notts and Derby passed to the British Electricity Authority, who in turn passed on the company in April 1948 to the BTC. The trolleybus services were abandoned in 1953, with the remaining AEC and BUT trolleybuses passing to Bradford Corporation, where many lasted, albeit rebodied, until the end of UK trolleybus operation in 1972. The last N&D trolleybuses were replaced by standard BTC double-deckers, 15 Bristol KSW6G buses with ECW H60R bodies, but in traditional, rather than Tilling-style, livery.

In April 1927 a 14-seat Chevrolet bus began working a route from Stratford-on-Avon to Shottery, the operator being Stratford-Upon-Avon Motor Services, a company formed by two local businessmen. Further routes were quickly opened,

Despite its front wings and radiator, this Rhondda bus is in fact an AEC Regent V, with a 61-seat MCW body, one of a batch of six delivered in 1956.

mostly in a south-westerly direction, including a service to Cheltenham. Although there was a route from Stratford to Leamington, expansion in that direction was restricted by the operations of the Balfour Beatty subsidiary Leamington and Warwick Electrical Co Ltd, and in fact, Stratford-upon-Avon Motor Services was purchased by the Balfour Beatty group in 1929. On 4 May 1931, **Stratford-upon-Avon Blue** Motors Ltd was registered as a direct subsidiary of the Midland General Omnibus Co Ltd, and at the same time some services in the Cheltenham and Evesham areas were passed to Bristol Tramways. However, in 1935 the Birmingham and Midland Motor Omnibus Co Ltd purchased Stratford Blue from the Balfour Beatty group, but operated the Stratford company as a separate entity. In fact, despite manufacturing its own vehicles, only three such BMMO-built buses entered the Stratford fleet, such was the autonomy of its operations. In 1940 Stratford bought its first, and until 1946, its only double-decker, but after World War II the company bought eight standard Leyland PD2 Titans, together with 10 single-decker Tigers PS1. PS2 Tigers later followed, and a quintet of these was rebuilt with double-decker Northern Counties bodies in the early 1960s. Stratford Blue buses maintained an extremely smart blue, cream and silver livery, which

gave the vehicles a very dignified air. The company was merged with the Midland Red parent on 31 December 1971, and the vehicles were sold, although many are still in service with other operators, such as Preston Corporation.

In 1926, there started near Cheltenham a small company running excursions during the summer to local beauty spots, under the name of **Black & White** Luxury Coaches Ltd. Within three years, express services were in operation, to places as far apart as Swansea and London, and the large Cheltenham coach station was opened in 1932. In 1934 a number of operators (Black & White, Midland Red, Red and White, Elliott Bros (later Royal Blue) and Greyhound (later Bristol Tramways) pooled their express workings to form Associated Motorways, Cheltenham becoming the hub of these operations. Naturally, the company's coaches were painted in a very smart black and white livery, with Bristol being the most popular chassis from 1936-1950. During the 1950s Willowbrook built bodies for the company on Leyland Royal Tiger, Guy LUF and AEC Reliance chassis, and then AEC became the standard with bodies by Duple, Harrington and Roe. In latter years the company bought a number of the none-too-successful Daimler Roadliner, and on passing to the NBC Black

North Western undertook a large rebodying programme of its prewar stock in the postwar period. This 1938 Bristol L5G carries a postwar Willowbrook body and PV2 radiator and wings. It is seen leaving Sheffield for Manchester.

& White became the mainstay of National Travel (South West) Ltd.

Turning to the south east, there were three London coach companies that have disappeared since, and as a result of, the formation of NBC.

Smallest of the BET companies was the grandiosely-titled **Redline** Continental Motorways Ltd, of Notting Hill, W10, which was a direct descendant of the pre-London Transport Red Line Omnibus Co, the coach side being developed after the bus services had been taken over by the LPTB. BET took over the company in the early 1950s.

In 1920, film producer George Samuelson began running coaches from London to various coastal resorts, under the name of **Samuelson** Saloon Coaches Ltd, and in 1925 the first express services were commenced, to High Wycombe, Oxford and Birmingham, and later to Liverpool. In 1931 a controlling interest in Samuelson's was acquired by the Red & White group who repainted the fleet in Red & White's livery. Soon

after, control of the company passed to London Coastal Coaches who passed the former Samuelson's express licences to associated companies. LCC, who owned and operated Victoria Coach station, reconstituted the company as Samuelson New Transport Co Ltd, and LCC eventually became a joint BET/BTC company via associated companies holdings, as did Samuelson's. The first postwar coaches arrived in 1951, in the shape of some Duple-bodied Leyland Royal Tigers in a pleasant cream and green livery, followed by 18 AEC Reliances with various styles (Britannia, Continental, Elizabethan, etc.) of Duple bodies, delivery of which was spread over seven years. Samuelson's provided transport from London to Gatwick for Transair Ltd, and when that company became part of British United Airways, a number of Samuelson coaches was painted into the smart blue, white and silver BUA colours, which Samuelson's later adopted as its own.

Synonymous with excursions from south-east

London for many years were the cream and maroon coaches of **A. Timpson** & Sons Ltd, of Catford, SE9. Alexander Timpson started his first motor vehicle excursion in 1912, although he had operated horse-drawn buses since 1896, but World War I bought his activities to a halt. However, Timpson resumed in 1919, and in 1920 he bought the former horse-tramcar depot of the South East Metropolitan Tramways Co at Rushey Green, Catford, and this served as the head office, coach station and garage. A bus service was worked with Tilling Stevens TS3A double-deckers between Plumstead and Bromley in the 1920s, but this was later sold to Thomas Tilling Ltd. Likewise, the local Timpson bus services in Hastings were sold to East Kent and Maidstone and District. A far-flung acquisition was in 1928 when control of the Torquay firm of Grey Cars took place, but this was sold in 1932 to Devon General. Alexander Timpson died in 1943, and in 1944 control of the company passed to BET (60 per cent) and Thomas Tilling Ltd, the latter holding passing to the BTC in 1948. After the war, a number of coach operators in the south east suburbs was acquired by Timpson's including Dartmouth Coaches, Forest Hill (1953), Bourne & Balmer, Croydon (1953), Homeland Tours, Croydon (1953). Bradshaw's Coaches, Plumstead (1957), A. Bennett, Croydon (1966), John Bennett, Croydon (1966) and A. Lewis, Farnborough, Kent, (1966).

Both Samuelson's and Timpson's together with Eastern National's coaching activities (themselves based on the former London coach operator Tilling's Transport (BTC) Ltd) became National Travel (South East) Ltd, but unsatisfactory trading results meant a restructuring of this entity, and NT(SE) ceased to trade as of 31 December 1978. Control of its express services in the south east passed to other NBC companies in the area, which gave London Country its first National Express workings, whilst a newly-constituted subsidiary, National Travel (London) Ltd, concentrates on London private hire and excursions, plus an expanding network of Anglo-Continental services.

In 1847, a 20-year old man laid one of the foundations of what eventually became the NBC. His name? Thomas Tilling, who started horse-bus operations so long ago. By 1900 Tillings was employing over 200 horse-buses in London, and was one of the first operators of the internal combustion engine when it put some Milnes-Daimler double-deckers on its Peckham - Oxford Circus route in 1904. By agreement with the London General Omnibus Co Ltd, the Tilling bus fleet to London was limited to 150 vehicles, so eyes were cast on other areas, a subsidiary being set-up in Hove, in 1915. As Brighton Corporation refused to license Tilling operations in that borough, his services ran non-stop from the Hove boundary to Old Steine, Brighton. However, this restriction was overcome when Tilling's purchased the local services of the Brighton, Hove & Preston United Omnibus Co Ltd, the country services passing to what became Southdown Motor Services Ltd. Thomas Tilling Ltd and Brighton Corporation concluded an agreement allowing the bus company to operate on specific routes which did not conflict with Corporation tram services. In 1926 the Woodingdean service of the Brighton Downs Motor Co was purchased, and in 1935 a new company was incorporated as a wholly-owned subsidiary of Thomas Tilling Ltd, this being the **Brighton, Hove & District** Omnibus Co Ltd. Brighton Corporation solely operated trams, apart from a brief foray into bus operation with hired vehicles in 1933. By 1937, the track was in need of renewal, and despite building new trams themselves, they were still open-top! However, in 1937 Brighton Town Council approved a scheme for pooling local services with BH&D, this being confirmed in a 1938 Act. Under this Act, the Corporation was to replace the tramway system with buses and trolleybuses, the Corporation operating $27\frac{1}{2}$ per cnt of the total vehicle mileage, with receipts being pooled and divided proportionally. A common fleetname, Brighton, Hove & District Transport, was adopted by the two operators, and a standard red and cream livery was applied to vehicles of both concerns. As part of its contribution to the trolleybus services, BH&D bought eight Weymann-bodied AECs, virtually identical to the 44 Corporation trolleybuses. However, the BH&D trolleybuses were stored during World War II, and did not enter service until 1946. BH&D lost its trolleybuses with Stage 1 of the Brighton Conversion scheme in March 1959, and in 1961 the two Brighton operators entered into a new working agreement with Southdown. With a much-enlarged operating area, the triumvirate became known as Brighton Area Transport Services, the proportion of route working and receipts-sharing being BH&D $50\frac{1}{2}$ per cent, Southdown 29 per cent and Brighton Corporation $20\frac{1}{2}$ per cent. BH&D came under Southdown control in 1969, and although maintaining its red livery, buses first carried a 'BH&D-Southdown' fleetname. Repainting of the fleet into Southdown green started in 1972 and into NBC green in 1974.

Wilts & Dorset Motor Services Ltd came into being as a result of the large number of military camps set up on Salisbury Plain during World War I, when it opened a service from Salisbury to Amesbury in 1915. In 1921, the Salisbury & District Co was acquired, together with the local services in the city, and in 1931 the company became a Tilling-British Automobile Traction associate, coming under direct Tilling control in 1942. British Automobile Traction was a BET-associate company. Early in 1910 BET, as a tramway operator, decided that the manufacture of buses did not usefully suit the company's purpose, but that the time was ripe for entering more extensively into motor bus operation, independently of tramways. The British Automobile Development Company therefore was made the basis of these operations. The name was changed to British Automobile Traction Co in 1912, whilst Thomas Tilling Ltd had acquired an interest in BAT itself. To co-ordinate and unify these varying interests BAT changed its name in 1928 to Tilling and British Automobile Traction, taking charge of the interests of BET and Thomas Tilling Ltd, in undertakings in which both had previously had their own separate interests. However, this only lasted until 1942. When the Red & White group was nationalised in 1950, its Basingstoke subsidiary, Venture Ltd, was put under Wilts & Dorset control, the vehicles being painted into Wilts & Dorset Tilling red livery, although retaining Venture Ltd on their legal ownership panel, as the licences were in this name. Control of Wilts & Dorset passed to Hants & Dorset in 1970.

In South Wales there was a group of BET/BTC subsidiary companies, which were merged into larger units, South Wales Transport taking Neath and Cardiff, Thomas Bros. and United Welsh, whilst Rhondda went to Western Welsh.

Thomas Bros (Port Talbot) Ltd was formed in 1951, when BET acquired four operators in that Glamorgan town, these being Afan Transport Ltd, Davies Bros Ltd, Thomas Bros Ltd, and Thomas and James Ltd, which companies had very mixed fleets of buses. This varied collection was operated for a couple of years, when a fleet of second-hand buses was bought from City of Oxford and Devon General. In 1954 some Saro and Weymann-bodied Tiger Cubs were purchased, the Leyland model being Thomas Bros standard bus chassis from 1954-63, whilst AEC Reliances were the choice for coaches. Three second-hand open-toppers came in 1960/1, two AECs, one each from Devon General and Eastbourne, and a Bristol from BH&D. Fleet livery was an attractive blue and cream.

United Welsh Services Ltd had been a part of the Red & White group, being formed in 1938 to consolidate the activities of a number of small subsidiary companies in the group, such as Gower Vanguard Motors Ltd, Eclipse Saloon Coaches Ltd, Enterprise Motor Services Ltd, Bluebird, Skewen and Neath Omnibus Co Ltd. These purchases brought a vast assortment of makes and models to the new company, prominent amongst which was the Red & White group standard, the Albion. During World War II utility Guy Arabs and Bedford OWBs were purchased, and then a postwar return to Albions. In the early 1950s a large Leyland fleet was purchased, with the first Bristols arriving in 1952, whilst 22 second-hand Bristol L saloons were purchased from Thames Valley in 1960/1 and 10 K6B/K5G double-deckers came from BH&D and Bristol. United Welsh also had the only Bristol SUL coaches not built for Western National, Nos 10/1 SUL4A/ECW C33F.

Neath & Cardiff Luxury Coaches Ltd fell into the BET net in 1952. Its main sphere of operation was an express coach service between Cardiff and Swansea, and although a fairly mixed fleet was operated, the company soon standardised on Guy LUF chassis, and later the AEC Reliance. The fleet carried an unusual brown and red livery, with the names of the towns served painted on to the vehicle sides.

In 1902 Rhondda Urban District Council obtained powers to construct and operate tramways, and in 1905 the Council leased the proposed tramways to the Tramways Development Company Ltd as trustee for the Rhondda Tramways Co. To further complicate this set-up, an agreement was concluded for the NEC to build, equip and operate the tramways; and yet another company was involved, the electricity coming to the system via the Rhondda Tramways Electric Supply Co Ltd. Eventually, on 11 July 1908, electric trams operated, and by the end of that year 50 cars were working 21 route miles, making it the longest system in Wales. In 1912 the Council asked the company to run a motor bus service to some newly-opened coalmines, but instead trolleybuses were used; however, severe road subsidence (a common hazard in coal-mining areas) caused the service to be curtailed after only three months, and the six Brush single-deckers were later sold to Teeside. Bus operation started in earnest in 1920, and the final trams ran in 1934, the company name changing to **Rhondda Transport** Co Ltd, with a fleet of 106 buses. Vehicles were mostly of AEC manufacture, with Leyland single-deckers in the postwar years, the livery being BET crimson.

Largest of these 'disappeared' companies was the **North Western** Road Car Co, of Stockport. NWRCC had its beginning when the BAT Company commenced bus operation in the Macclesfield area in 1913, and expansion was such that a wholly-owned subsidiary North Western, was formed in April 1923, which later became a Tilling-BAT subsidiary. In 1942, when there was a reorganisation of the holding companies, North Western went to BET control, its Tilling-BAT neighbour, Crosville, going to the Tilling group. However, vehicle policy was still largely Tilling-inspired, insomuch as the immediate pre-World War II standard were Bristols, both double and single-deckers, many more L-types joining the fleet until the 1948 Transport Act cut off the supply, for that Act

In its later days, Gateshead & District buses wore this green and cream livery. This Alexander-bodied Leyland Atlantean, seen in Gateshead in 1966, was one of seven delivered in 1964.

Sunderland District's smart dark blue and white livery worn by this Leopard/Marshall bus in 1966 disappeared into the anonymity of Northern General; Worswick Street bus station, in Newcastle, survives largely unchanged to this day.

restricted the sale of Bristol chassis, and ECW bodies, solely to BTC companies. Gardner-engined Atkinsons followed on from the Bristols, and then came Leyland Royal Tigers, Tiger Cubs and Leopards, the first of a large fleet of AEC Reliances were delivered in 1954, whilst 50 Dennis Loline double-deckers were bought in 1960/1. Further interesting buses were the 10 twin-steer Bedford VALs supplied in 1964; these were fitted with Strachans bus bodies of strange contour, to facilitate passing under a restricted bridge, later being replaced by Bristol RELL buses with ECW bodies to a similar design. Concurrent with the formation of the NBC, and as a result of the same 1968 Act, were the four passenger Transport Executives of Tyneside, Merseyside, West Midlands and South East Lancs./North East Cheshire (SELNEC). The latter covered an area from Alderley Edge to Whitworth, and from Westhoughton to Tintwistle, much of which was served by North Western. In fact, 60 per cent of

NWRCC services were in the SELNEC area. In November 1971 it was announced that SELNEC was negotiating to purchase the stage carriage network of North Western, and on 1 January 1972 the major portion of North Western passed to Crosville and Selnec, including depots and vehicles, the remainder passing to Trent. The coach fleet was left intact, and more than 80 vehicles were retained. In 1973 the company head office was moved to Preston, and together with Scout and Standerwick became National Travel (North West).

Many companies have disappeared as a result of NBC rationalisation, and new ones have been created, such as Alder Valley out of Aldershot & District and Thames Valley, and there will probably be other instances as bus traffic decreases and routes are pruned, forcing operators to amalgamate, to avoid unnecessary duplication.

The Continuous Passing Scene. The Plaxton Supreme body, here on Ford R1014 chassis, in the fleet of Barrie's Loch Lomond Coaches — against an appropriate background.

A Costly Mistake? Southport Corporation bought 12 of these Leyland Panthers with MCW bodies in 1968. One is seen in Southport in 1977, after passing to Merseyside PTE.

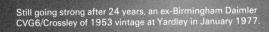
Still going strong after 24 years, an ex-Birmingham Daimler
CVG6/Crossley of 1953 vintage at Yardley in January 1977.

One Thousand and One ... or More

Waves, spots, stripes, bright colours, big fleetnames and, probably, one thousand and one different liveries are part of the Brazilian coaching and bus scene. Described by JOHN ALDRIDGE.

Above: I say one thousand and one because '1001' is the fleetname of a coach operator. His colours, seen here on a vehicle turning into Rio de Janeiro coach station, are relatively modest.

Trams can be found, after diligent search, in Rio, where a two-route system serving a hilly and difficult-to-approach-by-road part of the city has endured for years. Now track is being relaid and other improvements promised.

Brazil has few railways and one of the world's fastest-growing populations: three quarters of the people are under 30 years old. There is a popular saying that they came out of the trees and into their cars. And if they haven't a car but want to travel — and everybody does — it has to be by coach. There are licensing controls, and often routes are worked by a number of operators, each with their own timings. Coach stations are a busy, bustling part of a country almost as large as the United States of America, and whose population has jumped from 52 to 123 million in 30 years. Here coaches approach Sao Paulo's fabulous new station ready to load; in the background is the railway station, and on the right the unloading platform for terminating vehicles.

Coaches to Sao Paulo stay at ground level, but the passengers have to go up (by escalator) to an impressive first-floor concourse with shops, booking offices and restaurants, then down (by steps) to the numbered loading platforms.

Rear end design and logos are remarkable in Brazil. Our 1001 operator already seen has propellers superimposed on the '1's of his fleetname, no doubt to emphasise the 'turbo-superalimentado'. Having no rear windows gives added scope to the artist with his animal or other symbols, stars, stripes and anything else he might have thought of.

Electric traction can be found in some
parts, and Government-approved plans
envisage a vast trolleybus network.
Meanwhile, older trolleys soldier on in four
cities including Santos (*inset*) and Rio
(*main picture*).

The Rio tramcars, some dating from 1909,
are of cross-bench type with no internal
gangway. The fare is ridiculously low and
usually paid in incredibly soiled notes to the
roving conductor. En route the trams stop
for an inspector to look at the figure run up
by the conductor on a prominent indicator
inside the car — a once-common system in
some parts of the world. If he thinks the
figure likely, the car proceeds. Many
passengers don't pay anyway, but hang on
to the running board, jumping off each time
the car stops to avoid paying.

Some super luxury coaches can be found. Marcopolo built the body on this front-engined Scania chassis: two-and-one seating accommodated a total of less than 20 people, and the seats incorporated leg-rests as well as foot-rests.

Rather more passengers could be carried in the toilet-and-servery fitted Ciferal-bodied rear-engined Scania in the select private hire and touring fleet of Soletur Sol. Fleet numbering here, incidentally, is in fives to sound more impressive: thus coach 135 pictured was the next delivery after 130, and was followed by 140.

Articulated psvs, both buses and coaches, are the lastest idea in Brazil, as elsewhere. This is a Scania-Marcopolo front-engined coach, with bar and icebox, bottle holder, glass trays and a seat for the waitress on the articulation platform.

Above: Girlfriend in the foreground, overhead triangle in the background. In Bournemouth.

Right: View from an upper room: a trolleybus and its shadow. One of the 1958 Bournemouth Sunbeams.

Blissful Dreams of Long Ago

Bournemouth trolleybuses, and tramcars in Leeds and Sheffield, evoke fond memories for ROBERT E. JOWITT.

Dates ... dates in calendars and diaries ... not the squashy and edible sort of date ... though in passing it is interesting to note that, so legend has it, in the era when trams were plentiful and foreign fruits in round-ended wood and cardboard containers were cheap, boy scouts were instructed in the art of making a model tram out of a date box ... doubtless a very useful accomplishment. But as I say, I am not thinking about sticky delicacies, I am thinking about dates in calendars, thinking how every now and then a number and a month appear before my eyes and remind me that this is the *n*th anniversary of some momentous occasion in my life ... the first time I fell in love ... the first time I got drunk ... the last time I travelled on a tram in Leeds ... And I realise — with a shock — that these notable events took place 20 or more years in the past.

But still the hands of memory weave
The blissful dreams of long ago ...

... as the old song says. And even if, in the twenty or

more years which have elapsed since those dates I have frequently and in varying degrees of excess (or restraint) loved and drunk and ridden on such trams as remained when the Leeds trams were gone, and even if those subsequent sensations have overlaid many of my original impressions, nevertheless some of those early experiences (not necessarily blissful, actually) remain clearly in my mind.

Love ... It was at the height of Gina Lollobrigida's popularity ... An honorary-kind-of-aunt of mine had a girl from Genoa staying with her in Bournemouth. Apart from the fact that the girl had dark hair and brown eyes and was Italian, she did not bear, so far as I can recall, any striking resemblance to La Lollo. But she seemed to me very beautiful, and I began to suffer all the anguish of first love. (An anguish which, I believe, is spared the present generation of teenage lovers, who appear to have a licence and a boldness of which I would never have dreamed.) Anyway, in the course of one of the few brief meetings I had with her, she and I travelled on a Bournemouth trolleybus down from Christchurch Road to the Square, and another Bournemouth trolleybus back, I worshipping her silently and not daring to tell her so, in an aura of 1935-6 Sunbeam, with square-cornered windows (except at the rear), naked light bulbs in white holders, leather-like seats, and up-by-the-back-stairs and down-

98

by-the-front-stairs, the driver pulling the handle in the cab to operate the jack-knife front doors.

And despite my tongue-tiedness, and despite the fact that the girl soon returned to her native shores quite ignorant of my adoration, the 1935-6 Sunbeams retained for me for ever after a holy glow of rapture . . .

I had in fact seen the Bournemouth trolleybuses before I discovered Genoese beauty and the pangs of love, and I saw them many times thereafter. I first saw them in 1946, and thought them the last word in modernity. I continued to think that they looked very modern, even when I knew how old they were; which was 10 years old in 1946 and 20 years old when I fell in love on them. I still think that those Sunbeams were

some of the smartest and most ageless vehicles I ever saw. They looked no older than the BUTs of 1950, even though the latter had much more sumptuously fitted interiors with moquette seats and butter-dishes over the light bulbs. The Sunbeams still looked fine when they were being scrapped, by which time I was riding on the new Sunbeam trolleybuses of 1958-62 with one or another of several girls who followed in the wake of L'Italiana.

The hands of memory weave for me fairly clear pictures of all three generations of the yellow trolley-buses (and of the two-axle BUTs which came second-hand from Brighton as small sisters to the big Bournemouth three-axle BUTs) for the yellow trolley-buses formed so prominent a background to friend-

Square-cornered windows except at the rear, up by the back stairs and down by the front stairs, and out by the jack-knife doors.

ships with girls which were much more serious than an après-Lollobrigida idyll. The noise of the overhead heralding the otherwise almost silent approach of a trolleybus, the clunk of the booms passing under points, these made the accompaniment to impassioned declarations or intense arguments . . . blue sparks from the wires flashed to illuminate a halo of the prevailing feminine hairstyle or to be reflected in a pair of loving eyes . . . chips shared on the back-seat upstairs with a damsel from the art college had a special flavour . . .

I remember writing several pages of love-letter to a girl at a convent-school, describing in detail how a trolleybus dispoled at the Lansdowne, slipped back so its poles entangled themselves in the wires, and caused

a long queue of trolleybuses to build up behind it. The girl subsequently said she didn't want to see me again, but I never really discovered whether this was because I devoted too much of my love-letter to tales of dispoled trolleybuses, or for various other reasons too lengthy to detail here.

Some of my memories of Bournemouth trolleybuses are less clear. Vaguely I recall a scene of festivity in an upper room, and hurling a loo-roll over the trolleybus wires, but I cannot remember what effect it had. Was it so late at night that the trolleybuses had ceased running? Did the trolleybus poles scrape it off the wires in the following dawn, long after I was dead to the world, or had it blown away by then in the breeze?

The last night in Leeds. Spectral figures, and a tram which was about to be no more than a ghost itself.

I shall never know.

I have mentioned already that — obviously once a year — I encounter the date on which I was first inebriated. The occasion of the festooning of the Bournemouth trolleybus wires was far from being the first occasion where my memory proved hazy.

The date when I first looked upon the wine when it was red and learned that the affluence of incohol prevents you from walking straight was some two years after the Italian episode in Bournemouth. This time it was in Germany, and the wine was in fact white and not red, and, helped by the Westphalian beer, lost me the respect of a golden-haired maiden with brown eyes and a dark-haired maiden with a pony-tail and eyes

the colour of which I regret to say I no longer remember, though I continued to adore both these girls, as well as still adoring the Italian girl, for a long time afterwards. But the only background noises on this occasion, as the flat-fronted square-bodied Bussing single-deck buses of the Kraftverkehr Westfalen had already gone to bed, were the voices of Deutsche Bundesbahn steam locomotives on late night goods trains and I dare not make so bold as to describe the delights of these heard through the blur of liquor in the pages of a book devoted to buses. But I felt that having mentioned the moment when liquor first touched my lips, I could not leave my readers in ignorance of the details.

My readers, however, having now been satisfied on this point, may wish me to enlarge upon that other occasion I mentioned, my last tram ride in Leeds.

My last tram ride in Leeds was actually the last tram ride in Leeds for a great many other people too; I rode in the procession of several 'last-cars'. But I have memories of Leeds trams on several dates prior to this sad time, for even if I cannot claim such intimacy with the Leeds trams as I had with the Bournemouth trolleybuses, my father and I paid three or four visits to Leeds in the declining years of the trams, mainly for the purpose of riding on the system where he had been brought up when it was new and splendid. And therefore each journey on the Leeds trams was for me

something special, not an everyday matter like riding on the Bournemouth trolleybuses. Thus the sensations of crawling out through the bottom of Leeds to Hunslet or climbing up through the several styles and ages of domestic architecture marking the outward expansion of Leeds towards Moortown or charging dramatically down through Middleton Woods are fairly well fixed in my mind; and if I have had similar rides in other parts of Europe which have slightly confused my exact memories of Leeds, the other rides were not on the top decks of Horsfields or Felthams, and I remember, despite subsequent impressions, how different the two types seemed. Blissful dreams, certainly. But the memory which remains most

Left: A scene which could now only be found at a Crich Extravaganza — but this is how Sheffield really appeared in the late 1950s.

Right: A Feltham was always a Feltham, even in Leeds livery.

Below: Sheffield — trams . . . and more trams . . . and still more trams.

strongly is not so blissful, it is the sense of tragedy, of something precious and irreplaceable being torn away, as on that murky evening in November 1959 the trams came in one by one from Halton and Crossgates, never to come in again. That feeling of irrevocable and tragic parting survives with me yet, more strongly then the memory of actually riding on the tram in Leeds, as strongly as more awful partings from some of the followers of the original Italian girl . . . One such parting, it may be mentioned incidentally, had a background of Oporto tram noises (and narrow gauge railway steam whistles) and another started actually on a tram in Vienna . . .

But come! Am I not letting my nostalgia for long ago dwell overmuch on girls who are now probably married . . . (and with daughters fast approaching the age and beauty which their mothers had when electric cars still clanged through the streets of Leeds.) Let me turn to another Yorkshire tramway.

Let me turn to Sheffield. And though I have memories of Sheffield on the dreadful night when the last trams ran and the Heavens wept copiously, I have happier memories of Sheffield a year or so previously, when the trams, even if under sentence of death, flourished still in vast quantities, doing their duties faithfully and carrying vast quantities of passengers.

I remember various details . . . the trolley pole reversers on the overhead wire at certain termini . . . the terrific, almost switch-back gradients encountered on some of the routes . . . the variety of scenery from almost pastoral to heavily industrial . . . the motormen calling the newest cars 'pneumonia cars' because, although these Roberts cars were of very smart design and only seven or eight years old, their design was such that the wind whipped very draughtily round the front platform on to the driving position . . . But above all I remember the rush hour with streets full of endless thriving processions, trams and more trams and still more trams.

A little voice tells me that it is impossible, that it is only in such fairy-tale cities as Lisbon that this happens, such cities as are perhaps only a figment of the imagination. But I know it was so; that this vision of ceaseless trams, even if now it seems unbelievable, was once reality.

Such people as saw it will understand me. Those who never knew will never know.

They must accept that they can never find the fabric of the blissful dreams of long ago . . .

I suppose they will find their own magic, and build their own dreams, on such material as I might consider better fitted for the foundations of a nightmare . . .

But will anyone teach them how to build a model tram from a date box?

Left: King Street, Kilmarnock in 1950, and passengers board a Western SMT all-Leyland Titan TD5, dating from 1938.

Below: Greenock Motor Services, although a subsidiary of Western SMT, was operated as a separate entity until 1949. This Guy Arab/Weymann 55-seater was still in GMS livery in 1950.

Foot of page: Newly delivered to Young's Bus Service, Paisley, in 1950, this smart Daimler CVG6 with 56-seat Northern Counties body passed with the company to Western SMT in 1951. It is seen in Clyde Street, Glasgow.

Mr Smith's
Scotland

In 1949/50, the late ALLEN T. SMITH visited Scotland with his camera, and his photographs provide a memory of the buses and trams of the time.

Above: An Edinburgh Corporation Metropolitan-Cammell steel tram of 1934, in Princes Street in 1950 on a short-working to the Zoo Park.

Right: Argyle Street, Glasgow, with the arch of Central Station in the background, and passengers boarding one of the 1927 Hurst Nelson-built Kilmarnock Bogie cars.

Below: Time for a chat in Aberdeen. The conductor of a recently-acquired ex-Manchester Corporation Pilcher car passes time with the driver of a 1920 open-balcony car.

Top: Recently acquired from Sheffield Corporation, this Clyde Coast all-Leyland TD5c, dating from 1938, sits at Saltcoats before its journey to Largs.

Above: A 1935 ex-Ribble Leyland TD4 with lowbridge 53-seat English Electric body, bought by Alexanders in 1947. It is seen in Glasgow in 1950.

Left: In 1950 Alexanders bought the Sutherland, Peterhead, bus business. This 1945 Daimler CWA6/Duple, still in Sutherland livery, carries an Alexander fleet number plate in this 1950 photograph in Aberdeen. Fitted from new with platform doors, it lasted in Alexanders' hands until 1964.

A rare photo of an Alexanders Bedford OWB, with 32-seat SMT utility body, wearing dark red Perth City Transport livery. The Perth Corporation services had been acquired in 1934, and although the dark red livery was retained for Perth town services until 1962, the PCT fleetname was phased out after the War.

Below: Austin taxi meets Glasgow bus — the bus was a Corporation 1947 Albion Venturer CX19 with Roberts 56-seat body, seen in 1950.

From 1949 the Edinburgh-based SMT fleet changed from a blue to a green livery. This 1940 AEC Regal, with 39-seat Alexander body, is in cream and blue, while in the background is a utility Guy Arab, also in blue, at St Andrew Square, Edinburgh, in 1950.

The Continuous Passing Scene

My Concise Oxford Dictionary defines *Panorama* as: 'picture of landscape successively rolled out before spectator; continuous passing scene; unbroken view of surrounding region'. Panorama was the name chosen by Plaxton in 1959 for its latest coachwork style for underfloor-engined chassis. It could not have been better named, for the view out of it exactly accorded with the dictionary definition!

Whereas there was an almost sacrosanct and universally followed tradition, even with Plaxton, to utilise a five, six, sometimes seven-bay window arrangement, and always opening, the Panorama flaunted convention and startled the industry by boasting just three long main fixed windows each side. There was also a half window and small glass panel wrapping round the rear quarters to form part of the rear window arrangement.

At that time Plaxton products were not as widespread as they were to become — one would have put Plaxton somewhere down the list of British coachbuilders. The Panorama was to change all that in time, since it went on to become the most popular coach style on Britain's roads.

Plaxton developed a distinctive, but not beautiful, style through the 1950s. It started with the Venturer, which went through various changes before being replaced by the Consort in 1956. The Consort had a higher window line and revised front, otherwise was broadly similar. The rear was very much like the Venturer but side windows continued round the back quarters to flow unbroken in form into a three part back window, a Plaxton hallmark of the period. Subsequent Consorts reverted to the Venturer style grille and lower window line, and later gained a two-piece wrap around windscreen instead of the earlier four pane style. The 1959 Panorama kept similar ends as the Consort but a more purposeful air was achieved, with less visual interchange between side and front, through a less wrapped round windscreen and a continuous rain strip moulding round the front over the screen.

The much revised Panorama for 1960, which wore a simpler, cleaner front, was beginning to show signs of a very elegant, simple and plainly brutal style. A definite horizontal, thrust-forward look was there, helped by the forward protruding roof (incorporating air intakes for the forced

RAY STENNING considers the styling of the Plaxton Panorama coach body, and its descendants.

Top: An early Plaxton Panorama bodied AEC Reliance gets the signal to go at the 1959 British Coach Rally. It was in the fleet of Straws, Leicester, and was voted 'Coach of the Year'.

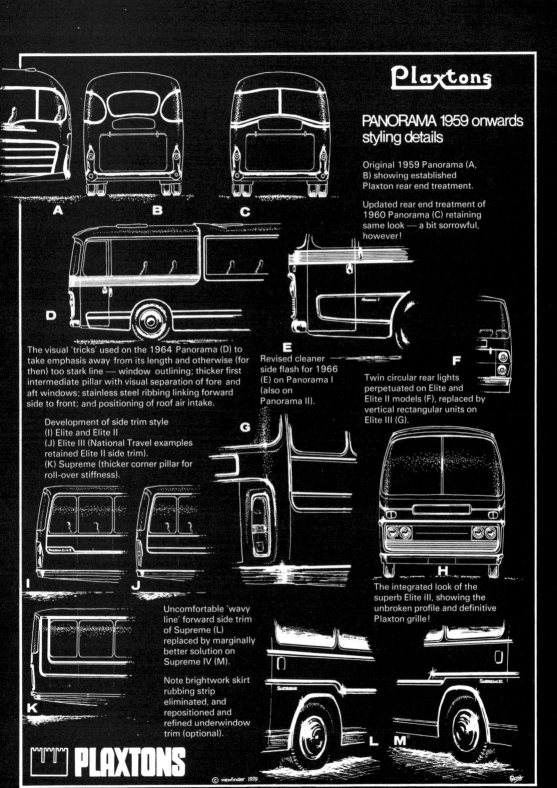

Plaxtons

PANORAMA 1959 onwards styling details

Original 1959 Panorama (A, B) showing established Plaxton rear end treatment.

Updated rear end treatment of 1960 Panorama (C) retaining same look — a bit sorrowful, however!

A **B** **C**

D

The visual 'tricks' used on the 1964 Panorama (D) to take emphasis away from its length and otherwise (for then) too stark line — window outlining; thicker first intermediate pillar with visual separation of fore and aft windows; stainless steel ribbing linking forward side to front; and positioning of roof air intake.

E

Revised cleaner side flash for 1966 (E) on Panorama I (also on Panorama II).

F

Twin circular rear lights perpetuated on Elite and Elite II models (F), replaced by vertical rectangular units on Elite III (G).

Development of side trim style
(I) Elite and Elite II
(J) Elite III (National Travel examples retained Elite II side trim).
(K) Supreme (thicker corner pillar for roll-over stiffness).

G

H

I **J**

The integrated look of the superb Elite iII, showing the unbroken profile and definitive Plaxton grille!

Uncomfortable 'wavy line' forward side trim of Supreme (L) replaced by marginally better solution on Supreme IV (M).

Note brightwork skirt rubbing strip eliminated, and repositioned and refined underwindow trim (optional).

K

L **M**

PLAXTONS

© viewfinder 1979

ventilation). The side windows, still three and a half bays, still continued round the back quarters to form the back window. A look similar to the previous Panorama back was achieved without the middle pane. The quarter panel windows swept round up into an ungainly arch with a thin pillar in the middle. Despite this rounded ugliness, it showed Plaxton's mastery at achieving the same look, the same effect, but updating it at the same time. Plaxton also built a version of the Embassy (which had replaced some Consort applications) for the underfloor-engined chassis, featuring the Panorama front.

When 36ft long vehicles became permissible during 1961, the Panorama was lengthened with an extra straight window bay inserted, giving a fussy appearance. Black & White's first Plaxtons, also its first 36-footers, were this style of Panorama. Somehow the length seemed to emphasise the falling windowline, a tradition of coach styling few yet had the courage to abandon completely. Harrington was first to do so with the Legionnaire in 1963, (although Alexander's straight-waisted Y type appeared in 1961), but Plaxton didn't eliminate it entirely until 1968 with the Elite.

In 1962 the Panorama, flushed with success, went for even bigger, longer windows. A four-bay arrangement (with the rearward one divided) was used and the earlier visual interchange between sides and rear done away with by straightening up the back and incorporating a conventional back screen. Also, the back end droop was all but eliminated — just a subtle fall in the waistline was kept to prevent the severe appearance that might have otherwise resulted. It's a trick used of old — the Greeks built their columns with a bowed profile to make them look parallel; it's a similar idea for the Panorama windowline. Now the panorama was a truly handsome coach with a beautifully clean look and purity of line. Traditional touches, like the side flash, hallmarked it a Plaxton. Unless you deliberately tried to isolate particular design elements, you just saw an overall concept expressed in metal and glass; the reasons I will explain later.

Southdown seemed to find this Panorama to its liking and has continued with Plaxton products since. Likewise Ribble, and many other operators. Because of the simplicity of line, the understated look, when some of these

1962/3 Panoramas received National white livery and markings they went through the transformation unscathed, even improved, whereas the subsequent version of the Panorama under the same treatment lost the effect of its looks.

While some die-hards were still boggling about the size of the current Panorama's windows, Plaxton went ahead and made them — impossibly some thought — even bigger for the 1964 Show model. Perhaps, however, feeling that the previous Panorama was a bit too plain and long looking, and this was off-putting to some customers, Plaxton decided to gild the lily and use a few tricks to deceive the eye. Also, maybe Plaxton customers were used to a bit of good clean tasteless ostentation, and their customers in turn similarly were partial to a bit of a swank.

By 'cutting off' the first side window through judicial use of pillar thickness and trim arrangement (also positioning of the roof ventilators), the eye was not so much tricked as instructed, but again so clever was the Plaxton solution that you still saw an overall visual entity. The broad stainless steel trim running below the first window and right round the front was not the vulgar expression it might have been. I'm not saying Plaxton were above that sort of thing — they weren't — but this did serve a purpose. The new grille and headlamp panel was in complete harmony with other styling elements and clearly derived from the superseded style, even if it was a bit gaudy. The 1964 Panorama made a sensational impact and drew many more customers into the

Ribble took to the 1962 Panorama, as here on a 1963 Leopard 49-seat coach leaving Edinburgh for Liverpool when new.

Plaxton net. It was showy, but that's exactly what the contemporary market wanted - and got!

In 1966 the lower side trim reverted to the more traditional Plaxton side flash (albeit stylised), which reduced the apparent height. This Panorama I, as it was labelled, was still a lovely clean, soaring style, in spite of the flashy trim. Supplementing the I, the Panorama II was introduced at the same time, intended mainly for the new Bedford VAM and Ford R192. Although it did away with the visual trickery of the Panorama I, it looked fussier due to sliding window toplights. This marked the introduction of a shorter Panorama, and both I and II were available in either 33ft or 36ft forms. Sometimes when fitted to Bedford's VAM or VAL the Panorama II was badged *Vam* or *Val*. At about the same time Panorama styling was extended to the Embassy for the Bedford SB and its like. The heavily-sloping front upset the look in that application.

Plaxton caused another sensation and broke fresh ground again, in 1968 with the all-new Panorama Elite. Viewed end-on the Elite's profile from skirt to cant was a perfect, unbroken, shallow arc. The curved side windows, flush fitting with radiused corners and an integral part of this smooth profile, made for increased shoulder room inside. The same even curve was repeated with the end contours, continuously bowed from bumper to roof, meeting the roof abruptly but naturally. The whole shape was natural, complete. Even without the grille panel perpetuated from the previous

Panorama, the Elite was still unmistakably a Plaxton: a superb piece of coach design — modern, uncontrived, elegant, distinctive, restrained. Plaxton was now at the top of the tree. Common body panels and standard window sizes enabled alternative length bodies to be made easily, based on a four-bay arrangement for the 10 metre version (four and a half on the 11 metre'.

The Panorama Elite II superseded this model two years later. Main external difference was a tidier lower front panel incorporating a slightly revised and better integrated grille and headlamp panel. 12 metre versions retained four and a half window bays as on the 11 metre model, but the main windows were, of course, longer.

As with any entity that develops a living evolving character over a length of time, there is bound to be a zenith at some point. That is not to dismiss what came before or what followed, but there is a point when almost everything is at its prime. Do you remember in the book by *Muriel Spark* (and film and television versions) Miss Jean Brodie was telling her girls that everything has its prime and that she was in hers? The Plaxton Panorama achieved its prime with the Elite III model in 1972. Most noticeable external difference was replacement of traditional (since 1964) double circular rear lights by single vertically rectangular ones. Contemporary Plaxton publicity heralded the Panorama Elite III as the world's finest looking coach. That was no idle boast. In line, in proportion, in detail, it was just right. Even now, nearly a decade later, it

The 1966 Panorama compared, both on Ford R192 chassis. On the left is the plainer Panorama II, with top sliding windows; alongside is a Panorama I, with the 'isolated' first main side window.

still looks just right.

The Panorama Supreme - badged simply, Supreme, without the Panorama prefix — was introduced in 1974 on the Bristol LHS and Bedford VAS (this marked the end of separate styles for different chassis), and as Supreme II in 1975 on the full-size chassis. The Elite had been going for six years and in age terms was due for replacement. The Supreme was an attempt to update the Plaxton line that didn't quite work; it was a bit clumsy.

The hallmark of the Panorama's aesthetic success over the years was the overall look, achieved by all design elements relating to the overall design 'intention', either by subtle echo, by emphasis, or by careful counterpoint, and it was a fine balance between them all. No single styling feature demanded more attention than another; the eye was never distracted from the overall effect. Except with the Supreme. The perfect profile of the Elite was replaced by a more practical shape but one that was uneasy on the eye. The Supreme looked top heavy and rather bloated. Its side mouldings had a double kick to them (on some versions, single), a flagrance of basic design principles (conflicting emphases cancelling one another). The front and rear screens were arched ridiculously at the top, giving a sorrowful look. All these things, even the over-ornate revised grille (often a characterful but vulgar Plaxton self-indulgence) demanded more attention than the overall look, and made the Supreme something of a self-parody.

It's unfair to dwell on the less happy aspects of the Supreme, especially as it continued the sales success of the Elite. With only Duple's Dominant a serious (but formidable) rival on the home front, and imports like the expensive but superb Van Hools and the Portuguese-built 'gin palaces' from Alf Moseley, to threaten its supremacy, it is hardly surprising. And Plaxton's customers are loyal. You could argue that discussion on its looks is all very subjective. I would disagree, from a professional viewpoint, and beauty being in the eye of the beholder is more a condemnation of the beholder than a statement about beauty! However, certain long overdue features were incorporated, like the practical rubbing strips running at bumper height right around the lower body sides. When manoeuvring a coach in tight spots, especially by low stone walls, it is very easy to graze paintwork at that height or push panels in.

Left: One of the United 12 metre Elite IIs on Bristol REMH6G chassis, built in 1971.

Centre left: One problem with high windows! Tatlocks Leopard with uneasy-looking Viewmaster body, at the 1976 Show.

Bottom left: Three Bedford/ Plaxtons in the fleet of Berry's Coaches, of Taunton. MYA is a VAM/Panorama I; VYB an early Elite, again on VAM; KYB an Elite II on YRQ.

A hideous-looking adaption of the Supreme was unveiled in 1976, the Viewmaster. This was a high floor model with an overall height of 11.5ft, but whether the British market will take to this continental idea remains to be seen, especially when body styles are merely 'jacked-up' versions of the standard product. Also in 1976 an all-metal version of the Supreme, the Supreme III was introduced in export and 12metre versions. It is interesting to note that some heavily-modified Supreme bodies were fitted to Mercedes-Benz chassis for Wahl, of Camberwell, which looked stunningly good.

Continuing its standard two-yearly cycle of minor or major revisions, 1978 marked the introduction of the Supreme IV, at the combined car and commercial Motor Show held for the first time outside London at the rurally-sited National Exhibition Centre near Birmingham. The Supreme IV featured a simpler, less heavy trim arrangement and revised grille. Twin vertically arranged rectangular headlights, incorporating side and indicator lights, flanked a grille opening of characterless shape. But it does show the start of a cleaning up of the Supreme. A new windscreen was of happier shape, but the back screen unaltered, strangely, and presumably economics dictated that the Viewmaster should retain its previous arched top windscreen. Don't let me give the wrong impression of the Supreme IV. It isn't bad looking at all, and shows the start of a return to the highpoint of the Elite III, but in terms of the 1980s. The Supreme IV is still unequivocally a Plaxton of the same line of evolution.

This evolution of the Panorama demonstrates more readily than any other body style how a design concept has been developed logically, naturally, over the years; each model a development from the last; each model furthering successful design elements, each shaped by contemporary feelings and fashions, by legislation and technical possibilities, but still unmistakably the same continuing line. The Panorama has been like another legend of the motoring world — Jaguar. The latest may look nothing like the first, but just as the XJS is every lean, hungry, arrogant inch a Jaguar, so Plaxton's newest models have resulted from a direct line of evolution stretching back over 20 years. With a bit of luck the Scarborough-based family firm will continue to develop that line and reflect, and one hopes, lead, the coaching world forward through the 1980s, 1990s . . .

Top: A Galleon Tours AEC Reliance demonstrates some of the points made in Ray Stenning's text.

Above: The Supreme IV, here on a Bedford YMT of Hill's, Stibb Cross, is cleaner in line and detail than its immediate predecessor.

One of Midland Red's converted Leopard/
Plaxton tow wagons, in yellow livery, tows
a new Leopard/Plaxton in white Midland
Red livery, so to speak.

A Lancashire United Leyland Tiger TS7,
new in 1937, with Roe body, tows a Guy
Arab UF/Weymann from Howe Bridge
depot in 1961. It became a towing vehicle
in 1956.

Converted from a former Strachan-bodied
single-deck bus, Aldershot & District
Dennis Lancet J3 No 38 comes to the
rescue of an ailing Dennis Loline I double-
decker in Bridge Street, Godalming in
1969.

A South Wales AEC Regent, converted for towing and tree-lopping, alongside an equally aged Regent, in 1952.

An Eastern Counties Bristol FS/ECW tow wagon rescues a Bristol RE at Copdock, near Ipswich, in 1978.

Two ex-Coventry Daimlers in the West Midlands PTE fleet — a CVG6/MCW tows a Fleetline/East Lancs in the centre of Coventry in 1979.

After decades of consistent growth, the British bus industry got a fright as it entered the 1960s. A maelstrom of inflation, dwindling revenue, and acute shortages threatened to overwhelm it, governments were resigned to a car-based future, so the industry had to put itself back on course. Many looked to Europe for inspiration, and sought salvation in the one-man operated standee single-decker.

Given that one-man double-deckers were not permitted until 1966, and even then were faced with considerable resistance, it was a fair assumption. But, the only 11 metre single-deckers available from 1961 had high floors and mid-engines and were a poor substitute for the double-deckers which were due to be ousted. Thus, the rear-engined single-deck citybus was born.

Bristol, still restricted to fulfilling British Transport Commission needs, was first off the mark in July 1962 with its RELL which, ironically, was by far the most successful of the species. It was the company's first long single-decker, and featured a low chassis frame, air suspension, a five-speed synchromesh gearbox mounted ahead of the rear axle, and a Gardner 6HLX engine rated at either 150 or 120bhp.

The prototype went to United Auto, and over 2,300 production RELLs and 10 metre RESLs joined state-owned fleets over the next 12 years. Most were bodied by ECW, but many operators took advantage of the availability of Leyland 680 engines, and some selected Gardner 6HLWs. Semi-automatic gearboxes, made available around the time of Bristol's 1965 open market emancipation, soon took the place of the awkward synchromesh units.

Daimler unveiled its offering at the 1962 Commercial Motor Show in the shape of SRD6, a prototype low-floor chassis evolved from the already successful Fleetline double-decker. This had a front radiator, and a horizontal version of Daimler's own 125bhp CD6 MkVIII 8.6 litre diesel. A production model was still two years away, but there was promising talk of a 150bhp turbocharged version and of Gardner options.

When it next made a Show appearance, as the Roadliner, all caution had been thrown to the winds, and a power unit new to the British industry was sitting vertically at the rear. The squat 9.6 litre Cummins V6-200 sat longitudinally under the rear

The industry's flirtation with rear-engined single-deckers was an unhappy episode. ALAN MILLAR tells the sad story.

A Costly Mistake?

bench seat, and developed a respectable 150bhp. Air suspension was fitted to the Potteries show exhibit, but many production models were fitted with unusual Metalastik toggle-link rubber suspension which did little to entice conservative busmen.

The Cummins engine was never a popular choice, even after it was derated to 135bhp, and the 1968 alternative of an 8.36 litre Perkins V8.510 150bhp unit did nothing to boost sales. Only 134 Roadliners, including demonstrators were built for the home market, 58 of them going to Potteries which got its last 10 SRP8s in 1969. The only other customers to place repeat orders were Bournemouth and Eastbourne which took eleven and three respectively.

Belfast brought 18, Darlington — out of loyalty to its Cummins factory — took 12, but cancelled a repeat order, West Riding and Chesterfield took 10 each, and smaller orders came from Wolverhampton, Sunderland, and AA Motor Services. Most led ridiculously short lives, and if any piece of hardware could have killed faith in rear-engined citybuses, it would have been the Roadliner.

AEC and Leyland were less daring, and employed much of the technology of their existing ranges for their 1964 Swift and Panther ranges. Both went for chassis frames which were stepped ahead of the rear axle to give a flat standee area with low step entrances and exits, and existing horizontal engines and semi-automatic gearboxes were mounted behind the rear axle.

The AEC Swift came in 10 and 11 metre versions with the 8.2 litre AH505 engine (derived from the AH470) rated at up to 145bhp. AH691 11.3 litre engines, rated at up to 165bhp, were offered on the 11 metre version. Belfast, Birmingham, and Sheffield took Swift 691s, while 665 essentially similar Merlins went to London Transport. By ordering 838 Swift 505s, LT helped boost UK Swift/Merlin sales to over 2,100.

Leyland's 9.8 litre 0.600 and 11.1 litre 0.680 engines could only be fitted to the 11 metre Panther, so something cleverer, but less successful, was done for the 10 metre Panther Cub. The 6.54 litre 0.400 rated, like the Panther's 0.600, at 125bhp fitted on to the shorter rear overhang, but even when turbocharged it was under too much stress to satisfy most fleet

Merseyside PTE inherited Liverpool's 25 Bristol RELLs, the only examples with Park Royal bodies, and had transferred 2009 to St Helens by 1977.

engineers. Only 94 Panther Cubs were built for the home market, compared with around 600 Panther buses.

Luckily for Daimler, the Roadliner disaster did not keep it out of the new market. Birmingham wanted 24 low floor single-deckers in 1965, and most certainly did not want anything so out of the ordinary as an American designed V6 engine. Instead, it took standard 9.5metre Fleetline double-deck chassis fitted with Marshall 37-seat bodies and Gardner 6LX engines.

The Birmingham buses may have been rather crude and overweight, but they did implant an idea in others' heads. First 10 metre, and later 11 metre single-deck Fleetlines were developed with bodies which incorporated seats over the engine compartment. While it was never a totally satisfactory answer — a batch on Tayside literally cracked open due to their uneven weight distribution — impressive sales were recorded with over 300 being built.

Leyland offered the Atlantean as a single-decker to anyone interested, but got few takers. Three Marshall-bodied PDR1/1s, similar to the Birmingham Fleetlines, went to Great Yarmouth, Portsmouth took 12 Seddon-bodied PDR2/1s, and Merseyside PTE got a pair of Northern Counties-bodied PDR2s ordered by Birkenhead.

Outside London, the big cities showed a briefer interest in the new vehicles. Liverpool bought 110 Panthers with MCW bodies and became the only big city supporter of the RELL by taking 25 Park Royal-bodied examples. Leeds went for 120 Swifts — the biggest provincial fleet of them — and 30 Fleetline single-deckers, the last arriving in 1971.

Manchester bought Panther Cubs and Panthers and experimented with turnstile fare collection, Newcastle and Glasgow took token batches of Panthers, and small numbers of Swifts went to Birmingham and Sheffield. None was really convinced of the standee single-decker's potential, and many of the buses were relegated quickly to quiet suburban routes as soon as double-deckers were back in vogue. And, with the exception of Glasgow, deckers were back with a vengeance in the shape of 10 metre Atlanteans, Fleetlines, and Bristol VRTs.

Single-deckers made their biggest impact in the smaller towns and cities where journeys are short enough for passengers to be prepared to stand during rush hours. Swift, Panther, Fleetlines, and RE all did reasonably well in these areas, and the greatest proportion of the 464 RELLs and RESLs built for non-nationalised undertakings went to this sector.

It was one of these operators, Sunderland, which was associated more than most with the wholehearted use of standee citybuses. Its late general manager, Norman Morton, joined the undertaking after a career in road haulage, and was determined to reverse the decline in business with a combination of flat fares, token-in-the-slot ticket machines, and flashy-looking standee single-deckers.

The 10 Daimler Roadliners bought by Chesterfield were fitted with Neepsend bodies. All have been replaced by secondhand Panthers. 'Out of the frying pan . . . ?

Morecambe & Heysham bought 10 AEC Swifts, seven of them with two-door Pennine bodies.

Few rear-engined city buses went to independents. This Plaxton-bodied AEC Swift was one of two Swifts in the York Pullman fleet.

Six Marshall-bodied Daimler Fleetline single-deckers, ordered by South Shields, were delivered to Tyneside PTE in 1971. Three were sold to Darlington in 1979 as Roadliner replacements.

119

Lincoln bought 25 Roe-bodied Leyland Panthers between 1967 and 1970. This 49-seater, seen beneath the city's cathedral, was delivered in 1968.

Portsmouth was the Leyland Panther Cub's best customer, taking 26 including this Marshall-bodied vehicle seen in 1973.

Ninety single-deckers, Panthers mostly, but also some RELLs, Swifts, and Roadliners, were ordered for delivery between 1966 and 1968, and all were fitted with Strachans and MCW bodies to a transatlantic design specified by the undertaking. Bell Autoslot self service ticket machines, similar to some which Morton had seen in use in Copenhagen in 1965, were fitted, and a 4d (2p) flat fare was introduced in September 1966 once the first Panthers and Roadliners arrived.

The new policy looked promising, but was a financial disaster to the tune of £197,000 after a year. Interestingly, part of the blame was laid on the higher fuel consumption of the new buses, and there was an £1,800 bill to lower the entrance and exit steps on 20 of them. The fare went up to 5d in August 1967, but the council decided two months later to go against Morton's advice and replace the scheme with an unsubsidised zonal fares scale. Morton resigned in a fit of pique and never returned to bus management.

Perhaps it was Tyne & Wear PTE's abolition of the zonal fare scale and tokens in 1974 and the gradual substitution of double-deckers for single-deckers in

Sunderland which heralded the death of the breed in Britain.

But there was still room in the market for another single-decker in 1969 when National Bus was increasing its orders for Bristol REs and demand elsewhere was outstripping supply. Seddon stepped in then with its Pennine RU, a Gardner 6HLX-engined mock-RE which ought to have been better than it was.

It did well at first, notching up a 100-vehicle order from Crosville, and one for 50 from Lancashire United. Such Bristol-starved municipalities as Blackburn, Accrington, and Burnley, Colne & Nelson pitched in with small orders, and Doncaster and Huddersfield showed faith to the tune of 24 and 23 vehicles respectively. But there were problems with chassis design and with bodies built by Seddon's coachbuilding subsidiary which demanded heavy warranty repair.

This must have reduced any profit earned by RU, and production ceased in 1974, by which time 273 buses had been built. Already, several have been withdrawn, and, despite its more attractive specification,

Three Marshall-bodied Leyland Atlantean 39-seaters were delivered to Great Yarmouth in 1968. Only 17 Atlantean single-deckers have been built.

The 50 Seddon Pennine RUs built for Lancashire United in 1970/71 have 40-seat Plaxton two door bodies.

the RU seems to have become another Roadliner.

By the mid-1970s, the chances of any first generation single-deck citybus were slim. Even such apparent single-deck converts as Blackpool, Great Yarmouth, Lincoln, and Preston were back with deckers, and the residual demand was satisfied almost exclusively by Leyland's advance specification National which has overcome many of the operating problems first thrown up by Panther, Swift, etc.

Leyland stopped building Panthers in 1972, and the last seven went, appropriately, to Preston. Fishwick of Leyland got the last single-deck Fleetlines (with Leyland 680 engines) in 1974, and Great Yarmouth got the last Swifts in 1975. Production of the RE was also supposed to end in 1975 with the delivery of a handful to South Wales municipalities and Merseyside PTE, but the needs of Northern Ireland dictated otherwise.

Ulsterbus and Citybus have launched on a policy to eliminate double-deckers from their fleets and are determined not to buy integral construction vehicles like the Leyland National. They have persuaded Leyland to keep the Bristol RELL in production to meet their needs and, by 1979, had bought over 340. They have also helped save the faces of other UK operators by acquiring their unwanted Swifts, Merlins, and single-deck Fleetlines as replacements for vehicles destroyed by rioters.

Other standee single-deckers have just been sold, either for scrap or cheaply in lots to dealers. Many of Liverpool's Panthers have gone, 18 of them to Chesterfield in place of Roadliners, Manchester's Panthers and Panther Cubs have long since vanished, some overseas, and the demise of the huge London fleet is a well-chronicled tale.

I doubt whether anyone could calculate how much the whole episode cost the industry, by the time extra maintenance costs, premature replacement, and lost resale value are taken into account. Add manufacturers' development expenses to that, and one could be excused for thinking that the industry lost more than it gained from going for standee single-deckers.

Night Out

The art of bus photography at night, demonstrated by the expert camerawork of T. W. MOORE.

Left: Reflections on a rain-soaked road during the Coventry rush hour in December 1976, with three West Midlands PTE ex-Coventry Daimler CVG6s.

Right: Driver Crump and Conductress O'Hagan have time for a cuppa at Leicester in January 1977, as their Midland Red D9 awaits its departure time.

A Weymann-bodied Leyland Leopard PSU3/4R of Midland Red leaves Corporation Street, Coventry, on the service back to Nuneaton in December 1976.

A Midland Red S21, working from Rugby depot, loads up for its return trip from Coventry. The ten-year old bus looked immaculate in this December 1977 evening scene.

Waiting for a bus in Derby Market Place in February 1977, but not for either of these Derby Corporation Roe-bodied Daimler CVG6s.

On a misty winter's night in Colmore Row, Birmingham, a 1963 Park Royal-bodied Daimler Fleetline of West Midlands PTE. In January 1977.

A Leicester Corporation Atlantean/Park Royal, one of eleven introduced in 1969, at Humberstone Gate in January 1977.

Depositing passengers in Derby Market Place in January 1974, a Trent ECW-bodied Daimler Fleetline in the evening rush hour.

Driver Edmund Smith poses with his coach,
a Black & White Duple-bodied Leopard just
arrived in Coventry Pool Meadow bus
station, in December 1976.

A cold night in February 1977 and a Trent
Leyland Leopard with Alexander T-type
body, about to depart for Belper.

A late night arrival at the De Vere Hotel, Coventry, for a Wallace Arnold Duple-bodied Leopard, in January 1977.

Overleaf: More of A. N. Wolstenholme's work from the 1940s and 1950s. First is the familiar cover illustration from many of the British Bus Fleets series, showing an anonymous Bristol/ECW Lodekka, and a Sunbeam/Willowbrook trolleybus, based on Walsall vehicles; Midland Red's 1944 D1 prototype, from the 1949 ABC of Midland Red Vehicles; from the 1957 Ribble ABC, a 1954 Leyland Tiger Cub/Burlingham Seagull coach; and from the 1957 London Transport ABC, one of the all-Leyland RTWs.

This Western SMT Seddon Pennine VII with Alexander Y type body had just arrived in Coventry on 23 December 1977 and would return to Glasgow with Christmas and New Year travellers.